SOCCER
A GUIDE FOR
PARENTS AND COACHES

SOCCER
A GUIDE FOR
PARENTS AND COACHES

U.S.O.C.
Sports Education Series

COOPER
Publishing
Group

Library of Congress Cataloging in Publication Data:

Author: Cooper Publishing Group

Soccer: A Guide for Parents and Coaches
U.S.O.C. Sports Education Series

Publisher: I. L. Cooper

Cover: David Schmitt   Copy editor: Kendal Gladish
     Gary Schmitt   Artwork: Craig Gosling

Library of Congress Catalog Card number: 96-96088
ISBN: 1-884125-54-9

10 9 8 7 6 5 4 3 2 1

*The Publisher disclaims responsibility for any adverse effects or consequences from the misapplication
or injudicious use of the information contained within this text.*

Contents

Acknowledgments

UNITED STATES OLYMPIC COMMITTEE

PRESIDENT
Dr. LeRoy T. Walker

VICE PRESIDENTS
Ralph W. Hale
Michael B. Lenard
George M. Steinbrenner III

SECRETARY
Charles U. Foster

TREASURER
Sandra Baldwin

EXECUTIVE DIRECTOR
Richard D. Schultz

DEPUTY SECRETARY GENERAL &
MANAGING DIRECTOR, BUSINESS AFFAIRS
John Krimsky, Jr.

CHAIR, COACHING COMMITTEE
Ray Essick

CONTRIBUTING EDITORS
Dr. Tom Crawford
Audrius Barzdukas

SERIES EDITOR   David L. Gallahue

As the Series Editor for the U.S.O.C. Sports Education Series, Dr. Gallahue has provided the expertise and guidance for the development of this book and the others in the Series. His personal and professional commitment to children made this Series possible.

David L. Gallahue is Professor of Kinesiology at Indiana University in Bloomington. He holds degrees from Indiana University (B.S.), Purdue University (M.S.), and Temple University (Ed.D). Dr. Gallahue is active in the study of motor development, movement, sport and fitness education of children. He is author of several textbooks, numerous journal articles, edited book chapters and films. Dr. Gallahue is a Past President of the National Association for Sport and Physical Education, former Chair of the Motor Development Academy, and the Council of Physical Education for Children. He is internationally recognized as a leader in children's motor development and developmental physical activity. He travels widely and has been an invited speaker, visiting professor or guest lecturer at over 200 colleges, universities, professional meetings and school districts throughout the world.

David lives on a small farm with his wife Ellie and several horses. He enjoys weight training, snow skiing, hiking, and climbing. He has two adult children, David Lee Jr., and Jennifer.

UNITED STATES SOCCER   *Special thanks to the following people at U.S. Soccer for making this book possible:*

Glenn Myernick, U.S.S. Coaching Coordinator for reviewing, revising, and providing expert advice. His love for the game, and children, helped keep this book on target. **Dan Gaspar** for his thoughtful review of the goalkeeping chapter. Finally, to the millions of soccer **players, parents, and coaches** nationwide whose participation has helped make soccer great.

AMERICAN COLLEGE OF SPORTS MEDICINE

The ACSM provided expert review of the injury prevent and treatment chapter.

Established in 1954, the American College of Sports Medicine has grown to more than 16,000 members in more than 75 countries, each dedicated to improving the quality of life for people around the world.

ACSM's mission statement reflects this goal: *The American College of Sports Medicine promotes and integrates scientific research, education, and practical applications of sports medicine and exercise science to maintain and enhance physical performance, fitness, health, and quality of life.*

ACSM's diversity and expertise makes it the largest, most respected sports medicine and exercise science organization in the world. From astronauts to athletes to those people chronically diseased or physically challenged, ACSM continues to look for and find better methods to allow everyone to live longer and more productively.

For more information on the ACSM, please visit the ACSM Home Page on the World Wide Web at *http://www.acsm.org/ sportsmed.* Or, you can receive information about the importance of physical activity and health by sending a business-sized, self-addressed envelope—with first class stamps already affixed—to ACSM National Center, Public Information Dept. U., P.O. Box 1440, Indianapolis, IN 46206-1440.

About the United States Soccer Federation

The United States Soccer Federation, or U.S. Soccer, is the national governing body of soccer in the United States. With headquarters in Chicago, U.S. Soccer served as host federation for World Cup USA 1994, the most successful event in FIFA history.

U.S. Soccer was one of the world's first organizations to be affiliated with the Federation Internationale de Football Association (FIFA), soccer's world governing body, beginning in 1913. U.S. Soccer has continued to grow and now has the second-largest membership among U.S. Olympic Committee national governing bodies.

The first International soccer games to take place outside the British Isles were between the U.S. and Canada in 1885 and 1886, respectively, almost three decades prior to U.S. Soccer's formation. Soccer in the United States has come a long way since then.

Approximately 50 full-time U.S. Soccer employees work to administer and serve a membership located in all 50 states. Known originally as the U.S. Football Association, U.S. Soccer's name was changed to the United States Soccer Football Association in 1945 and then to its present name in 1974. U.S. Soccer is a non-profit, largely volunteer organization with much of its business administered by a national council of elected officials representing three administrative arms—approximately 3 million youth players 19 years of age and under; 300,000 senior players over the age of 19; and the professional division.

U.S. Soccer manages seven full national teams. Men's programs include the National Team, Under-23 (Olympic), Under-20, Under-17, and Five-A-Side (Futsal). Women's teams include the National and Under-20 teams. Three developmental national team programs include Under-18 and Under-16 Boys and Under-16 Girls.

The host national association for the 1996 Olympic soccer matches, U.S. Soccer is proud of its many recent successes. The Women's National Team produced the most significant achievement in U.S. Soccer history, winning the first-ever FIFA Women's World Championship in China in 1991. The Women's National Team captured the 1994 CONCACAF title to qualify for the 1995 world championship tournament in Sweden, where the team placed third, falling to eventual champion Norway 1-0 in the semifinal. The U.S. squad won U.S. Women's Cup '95, exacting a measure of revenge with an overtime victory over Norway in the final match.

The Men's National Team won the U.S. Cup '95 title and advanced to the semifinals of Copa America before bowing out to world-champion Brazil 1-0. The Men's National Team advanced to the second round of World Cup play in 1994 for the first time in 64 years.

Other recent U.S. Soccer achievements include the Indoor National Team capturing the silver medal at the FIFA Indoor Five-a-Side World Championship in November 1992 in Hong Kong; the Men's National Team being crowned CONCACAF Gold Cup champions in 1991, winning the inaugural U.S. Cup '92 and defeating England 2-0 in U.S. Cup '93; the U-20 team finishing eighth in the 1993 FIFA Youth World Championship in Australia; and the Women's National Team finishing second in the 1993 World University Games in Buffalo, N.Y.

Coaching schools are held regularly throughout the U.S. where interested persons may gain certification at six progressive levels. U.S. Soccer has more than 72,000 certified coaches. The referee program makes up an integral part of the United States soccer scene, with approximately 74,000 referees currently registered.

Foreword
United States Olympic Committee

The United States Olympic Committee is very pleased and excited to celebrate the release of the Olympic Sport Education Series. This series is the result of a unique partnership between the United States Olympic Committee, its sport National Governing Bodies, and top-notch child and sport-skill development experts.

In a fun, easy-to-read format, it provides the information necessary to help parents and coaches give children a positive, healthy and developmentally sound experience in a wide variety of Olympic Sports as well as help families get involved with the Olympic movement.

The United States Olympic Committee places a high priority on seeking ways to enhance the sport opportunities and experiences of America's children. This series will help foster a high quality early experience in sport, which is associated with lifelong participation in sports and other healthy activities. The series will also help parents—the largest population of coaches in the United States—guide their children's participation, and feel comfortable and confident helping their children develop their skills in a fun, success-filled environment.

Good luck to all families and children who are beginning their pursuit of one of America's greatest opportunities . . . the Olympic Dream.

Dr. Tom Crawford
Director of Coaching
United States Olympic Committee

Foreword
United States Soccer

As the 1996 Olympic Games approach, the U.S. Soccer Federation is working diligently, in conjunction with the IOC, FIFA, USOC and ACOG to produce the best Olympic soccer competition in history.

Atlanta 1996 will mark the beginning of a new era in our sport when women's soccer debuts as a medal sport. U.S. Soccer proudly boasts of one of the best women's programs in the world, and our team has set its sights on a gold medal.

Our men's program has established high goals, as well. An excellent performance in World Cup USA 1994 has raised expectations of our men's Olympic team, which at a minimum wants to reach the medal round in 1996.

Soccer is the world's game, played by almost 200 nations. FIFA, the international governing body, has more members than the United Nations. Soccer is growing at a rapid pace in the United States, approaching 20 million participants. Nearly 75 percent of the participants are youths under the age of 19.

U.S. Soccer's primary goal is to foster the continued development of our sport in the United States. Thanks to the dedication of our staff and the thousands of volunteers who contribute their time and energy, we are well on our way to becoming a pre-eminent sport in the U.S.

Whether you are a soccer player, coach, referee or fan, I hope you will consider the benefits of joining U.S. Soccer, if you haven't already, and I am certain you will enjoy reading the *USOC Sport Education Series book on Soccer*.

Hank Steinbrecher
Executive Director/Secretary General
U.S. Soccer

1
Soccer: The Benefits of Participation

SPORT AND THE OLYMPIC IDEAL

Citius, Altius, Fortius. The Olympic motto expresses the desire of all athletes, whether they are elite performers at the Olympics or young hopefuls playing on local teams. All share the common dream of being *Faster, Higher, Stronger.* The Olympic creed first expressed more than 100 years ago by Baron de Coubertin, founder of the modern Olympic Games, is still the essence of all sport:

The most important thing in the Olympic Games is not to win but to take part, just as the most important thing in life is not the triumph but the struggle. The essential thing is not to have conquered but to have fought well.

At each Olympic Games one athlete is selected to take the Olympic oath on behalf of all competitors. Standing on the rostrum, the athlete holds a corner of the Olympic flag in the left hand, and with the right hand raised, speaks the following promise for all the world to hear:

In the name of all competitors, I promise that we shall take part in these Olympic Games, respecting and abiding by the rules which govern them, in the true spirit of sportsmanship, for the glory of sport and the honor of our teams.

The *motto*, the *creed*, and the *oath*, all represent the true Olympic ideal. An ideal that is no less important in your child's youth sport experience. An ideal for you, your young athlete, and his or her coach to remember. An ideal to embrace and to live by "for the glory of sport and the honor of our teams."

SHOULD MY CHILD PLAY SPORTS?

Organized sport has become an important part of American life. Today, it is estimated that more than 30 million American youth from ages 6 to 18 take part in one or more forms of organized sport.

This chapter examines the benefits of youth sport participation: **building self-esteem, positive socialization, developing character,** and **concept learning.** But first, let's talk briefly about the importance of making sport fun for today and enjoyable for a lifetime, and keeping competition sane.

Fun for Today

The number one reason children give for joining a youth sport team is to have fun. Keep this in mind when signing your child up. Kids are eager to make new friends, play hard, learn new skills, and increase their physical fitness, but they want to have fun in the process.

Sports for kids must make learning enjoyable and promote sane competition in a supportive environment. If the youth sport program fails to do so, players will become discouraged and eventually drop out. Of the estimated 30 million taking part in youth sport programs, almost 80 percent drop out by age 12. The number one reason—it isn't fun anymore.

Are We Having Fun Yet?
Questions for Young Players:

- What did you do at practice today?
- What new things did you learn?
- Did you learn anything to help you next time?
- Did you do your best?
- Did you have fun?

Enjoyment for a Lifetime

When helping your child choose a sport, consider its potential for lifetime benefits. Can this sport be played as a lifetime leisure, fitness, and fun activity? Or is it limited in its lifetime potential? Football, baseball, and basketball, although hugely popular team sports, are frequently limited in their lifetime potential. Sports such as tennis, swimming, golf, and track have excellent lifetime appeal. You could help your young player select basketball and tennis, or soccer and swimming as her sports outlets. She will have not only the benefit of participating in a team sport, but also the opportunity to develop skills in a sport that she can participate in for years on a recreational or a competitive basis.

Keeping Competition Sane

To compete is to pit your skills against an opponent, to try your hardest, to do your best, and to enjoy the chance to test yourself.

Competition is the lifeblood of sport, but it involves more than winning or losing. Sane competition inspires young players to give their best within the established rules. Sane competition rejects the win at all cost philosophy of some parents and coaches, and recognizes that kids are much more interested in playing the game than in determining a winner. Sane competition recognizes that cooperation, teamwork,

fair play, and sportsmanship are essential ingredients with lifelong implications.

Impact of Coaches

I have come to a frightening conclusion.
I am the decisive element on the playing field.
My personal approach creates the climate.
My daily mood makes the weather.
I possess tremendous power to make a player's life miserable or joyous.
I can be the tool of torture or an instrument of inspiration.
I can humiliate or humor, hurt, or heal.
In all situations my response decides whether a crisis will be escalated or deescalated and a player humanized or dehumanized.
—An Adaption of Haim Ginott

Parents and coaches working with children need to be accepting in a competitive environment. There is no place for teasing, sarcasm, or criticizing. Wise parents and coaches help young players set reasonable expectations for the game and the season that do not focus just on winning or losing. For example, a soccer coach may encourage players to set a game goal of allowing no more than 10 opponent kicks at the defender's goal, or not being offside more than once each period. Season goals might be to give maximum effort in each game, to win half the games, or to be in the top half of the division.

BUILDING SELF-ESTEEM

Parents and coaches are in a great position to influence the self-esteem and self-concept development of young athletes. Most kids place high value on being good at games, sports, and other physical activities. Positive self-concepts help players interact effectively. Sport can help young players view their world as manageable.

Self-concept is the sum total of your child's personal feelings of competence in physical, mental, and social settings. This self-description influences all that she or he does. Young athletes learn much about themselves as they respond to physical, social, and mental challenges.

Self-esteem is your child's estimate of how he or she is seen by others. Self-esteem is a powerful personal assessment of self-worth and perceived competence. Everyday experiences dictate whether children view themselves as competent or incompetent, worthy or unworthy.

In many ways, your child's level of self-esteem determines what he *expects* to happen, whether it is positive or negative. For example, players whose performances do not match their personal goals tend to see themselves as inferior, no matter how high their attainments may be. Conditions that may expose personal weaknesses are a major cause of low self-esteem.

Being good at games, sports, and vigorous physical activities contributes greatly to the development of both self-esteem and self-concept. Your child's coach should encourage these essential ingredients:

- a sense of belonging
- seeing oneself as competent
- believing in oneself
- having an inner sense of worth
- accepting oneself
- celebrating individual uniqueness
- living by a personal code of conduct

A Sense of Belonging

Belonging is the positive feeling your child experiences as a member of a group. It is the sense of being valued as a member of the team. Not only is it necessary for the team to regard her as belonging, she must regard herself as a legitimate member. Coaches do many things to help:

- use first names
- recognize something positively unique about each player
- require players to wear team hats, shirts, or shorts
- recruit competent adults to help and give them specific directions
- take and distribute team photos

Parents should volunteer often. Offer to help the coach teach certain skills or serve as a referee. If you are not familiar with your child's sport, arrange for uniforms, telephone trees, snacks, or team photos. Do anything that helps the coach focus only on building the skills and spirit of the team.

**Tips for Developing
Player Self-esteem:**

- *Practice "active listening."*
- *Give players plenty of eye contact.*
- *Smile!*
- *Avoid giving orders; ask questions to check for clarity and understanding.*
- *Don't put players in boxes with labels and then pay attention to the boxes.*
- *Promote player success, reduce opportunities for failure.*
- *Remind players of past successes.*
- *Recognize, accept, and appreciate differences in players.*
- *Emphasize player effort. Say, "You can be proud of . . . ," rather than "I am proud of you."*
- *Avoid artificial praise.*
- *Be sure that players clearly understand your expectations of them.*
- *Help players understand, accept, and express their feelings.*
- *Avoid hovering. Lead players toward independence.*
- *Practice unconditional acceptance of players for their innate worth.*

Coaches Help Players Feel They Belong By:

- *Structuring appropriate fitness and skill-building experiences*
- *Breaking skills down from complex to simple*
- *Maximizing each player's potential for success*
- *Personalizing their instruction*
- *Helping players set high but achievable goals*
- *Providing sincere encouragement*
- *Taking time to listen*
- *Making activities challenging and fun*

Seeing Oneself as Competent

Competence is how efficiently someone accomplishes a specific task. That "I can" attitude of self-assurance is evident in capable kids. Your child's perception of competence is a personal evaluation in comparison to others and to previous experiences. She sees herself as competent when she achieves personal goals or demonstrates individual improvement.

Competence is situation specific. For example, a young athlete may see herself as competent in soccer and basketball but incompetent in swimming and gymnastics.

Belief in Oneself

Competence is closely linked to confidence. Confidence is an inner feeling of *belief* in oneself. It's the notion that "I think I can." Children with self-confidence believe in themselves and their potential for achieving success. Wise parents and coaches help young players put negative events, such as failing to make a play or losing a race, into proper perspective.

Young athletes must have confidence in order to see themselves as competent. Developing sport skills and improving levels of physical fitness contribute greatly to self-confidence.

Youth Sport and Self-Concept Development

Self-concept
"How I see myself"
↑
Self-esteem
"How I think others see me"
↑
Self-confidence
"I think I can"
↑
Competence
"I can"
↑
Perceived competence
"I'm good at _____"
Youth Sport

An Inner Sense of Worth

Your child's personal sense of worth develops out of seeing himself as deserving and valued because of the kind of person he is. He believes that "I count."

Some coaches convey dissatisfaction by yelling, screaming, and using sarcasm. They share few positive observations and make players feel incompetent. Such behavior is unacceptable. Faced with such a situation as a parent, you need to decide *how* to intervene, not *if*.

First, observe your child at practice. Compliment your player's performance, reinforcing such things as hustle, teamwork, and skill improvement. Then talk privately with the coach. After praising his dedication, deal directly with the negative coaching behavior. Be calm, offer suggestions, and if possible volunteer your assistance. Most coaches will make conscious efforts to change. If not, take the matter to the next higher level with a reasonable demand for improvement.

Be careful in these situations. Anyone can have an off day. If a coach flies off the handle but later apologizes to the players, let the matter rest. If the coach has good reason to be upset with a player's behavior or broken team rules, back up the coach's authority. Help the coach by convincing your player of the need to conform to team codes of conduct. Get your child to practice on time, reinforce training rules at home, and support the coach's efforts to instill self-discipline.

Always remember to express your appreciation for the coach's interest and hard work, and encourage your child to do likewise.

Watch for Wounding Words

An adult's words to a child can hurt, heal, help, or hinder self-esteem. Even benign statements after practice such as "You sure got beat on that play" can do some damage. Acknowledge the disappointment over a missed play or lost game and help your player take two more steps:

- *learn from mistakes*
- *get over mistakes*

Self-Acceptance

To be self-accepting, children must understand and adjust to both positive and negative traits in themselves, and learn how to deal with them effectively. This may be difficult for young athletes who often have a right-wrong, good-bad view of the world.

Young players don't have a natural basis for realistic self-assessment and evaluation of others, so they tend to be overly harsh. If the child is dealing with true failure, the coach should emphasize improvement and learning which may transform a personal or team failure into an experience that builds the team's sense of identity and cohesiveness.

Every child should be able to find some degree of success and accomplishment in a sport experience. For some kids, success may simply involve getting into the game, making a good play, or making a goal. For others, it may involve making a spectacular play or being on the all-star team. Success should never be measured solely by a team's win-loss record.

Look for accepting coaches who are concerned about their players first and the game second. Such coaches are generally loyal sources of affection and support. They express acceptance in a variety of ways, especially with expressions of interest and concern. Look also for actions that convey an attitude of unconditional acceptance of young athletes for *who* they are, not for *what* they are.

One of the most potent ways to teach children to accept themselves is to demonstrate personal self-acceptance. Coaches can permit players to see how they deal with their own weaknesses. For example, when repeatedly miss-hitting a soccer goal kick during a practice demonstration, the coach could say, "I never was very good at making goal kicks, but I really love to kick the ball." Coaches who demonstrate personal self-acceptance help players see themselves in a more positive light.

Honoring Uniqueness

The entire idea of youth-centered coaching is based on treating young players as individuals. Players must learn to recognize and accept their unique qualities. Coaches who are attentive to their players also recognize unique abilities and structure practices and game plans accordingly. They allow for individual differences in experience, skill level, body type, fitness, and motivation. Within such a structure, all players recognize that they have legitimate places on the team.

A Personal Code of Conduct

For a child, virtue involves operating in accordance with an established code of behavior that is consistent with the expectations of her team, her culture, and her background. In a sport setting, that code of conduct takes the form of respect, loyalty, fair play, honesty, and responsibility.

Players need to know that virtue is a basic requirement of civilized society. Coaches who expect and help their players to act in such a manner contribute to the development of a positive self-concept. The group setting of athletic experience is an excellent place in which to learn to operate within a consistent code of conduct. Clearly defined and fairly enforced rules for acceptable behavior outline adult expectations.

POSITIVE SOCIALIZATION

Positive socialization is a process by which players modify their behavior to meet the expectations of the coach and teammates. Each player learns the rules and skills of functioning as a member of the team. As players are socialized into a sport they have opportunities to experiment with various social roles within the team, and to adopt behaviors that fit in with them.

Learning Appropriate Social Roles

Young players have many social roles. Although they gain some status simply by being members of the team, they also have different levels of status within the team. A player may be identified as an all-star player, bench warmer, hard worker, or lazy player and behave accordingly.

A role is a form of behavior used to carry out a particular status. For example, you may notice how much more mature your son or daughter acts on the team than at home. Your child's "job description" (status) on the team interacts with his or her "interpretation of the job" (role) and produces surprisingly mature behaviors. Behavior on the team is determined by certain norms or acceptable standards.

Coaches Improve Player Socialization Skills Through:

- *Effective communication*
- *Positive motivation*
- *Serving as role models*
- *Positive encouragement*
- *Rewarding effort*
- *Reducing the stress of competition*

Adopting Acceptable Team Behaviors

An acceptable standard of behavior is expected of each member of a team regardless of her individual status on the team, or her perception of her role. As players become socialized into their respective sports they learn acceptable and unacceptable behaviors in a variety of settings. Participation in sport occurs in a social setting involving teammates, coaches, and officials. Such a social setting requires players to make right decisions about both cooperative and competitive behaviors.

Making Right Choices

Socialization goes beyond players merely conforming to their status, roles, and norms. It's a process that requires both reasoning and social decision making. One of the primary goals of sport is to develop a sense of unity commonly called "teamwork" by working together for a common goal. Teamwork requires cooperation, effective communication, mutual compromise, individual honesty, and fair play.

In the social setting of sport, young players can learn to receive and give positive encouragement, develop the ability to realistic assess their abilities, and engage in group goal setting.

Receiving and Giving Encouragement

Encouragement takes many forms and ranges from self-encouragement to encouraging others. Kids need to learn that it's okay to feel good about their successes in sport. To teach self-encouragement, you can encourage yourself verbally in front of your young athlete. This is difficult to do because most of us are taught not to brag or to draw attention to ourselves. You can begin self-encouragement by expressing self-satisfaction in minor accomplishments when playing with your child. For example, when shooting hoops in the backyard you might say, "I really felt good when I made that basket." Or when helping coach your daughters soccer team you may say to her, "It made me feel great to know that I helped design the play used to score that goal."

Try the "Sandwich" Approach When Encouraging Players

- *First, find something good about the effort or the performance and tell the player ("Your kicking is looking much better").*
- *Second, provide an instructional cue. ("Remember, follow through in the direction that you want the ball to go").*
- *Third, encourage the player with a positive statement. ("Keep up the good work: you're making real progress").*

Coaches can begin teaching self-encouragement with things that are not highly personal. Group encouragement such as, "The team did a great job" or "Our team can do it," may be effective. Question-asking is another tool. If a coach asks "Don't you think you did well on that?" the player has a chance to say something personally positive. At some point the coach should move into more personal qualities so that players begin to see that it's helpful to say nice things about themselves as individuals.

Parents should follow the coach's lead in giving positive encouragement in specific small areas of good and poor performance. Young players need to hear positive statements from you that temper failure with realistic hope for the future. "Wow! What a super effort. You're really getting the idea."

Goal Setting

When helping players set performance goals ask yourself:

- *Are their goals reasonable?*
- *Are their goals achievable?*
- *Are their goals individualized?*
- *Are their goals generalized?*

Goal Setting

Goal setting must be individual. It must be made in relation to past performance, and it must have an end in view. If a coach wants players to commit to a goal, the players must help set the goal, and parents must provide support. The goal should exceed previous achievements, but only slightly. The goal may be far below the eventual performance level toward which the team is striving, but a lower level is reasonable because it is attainable. Meeting incremental goals gives reinforcement on the way to achieving larger ones.

As a parent of a young player it's important for you to support both individual and team goals. Make sure, however, that you don't become a focal point in the goal-setting process.

CHARACTER DEVELOPMENT

Sport has tremendous potential to promote character development and to teach the virtues of hard work, respect, honesty, teamwork, loyalty, self-control, and fair play. Talent may get a player on the team, but character will determine how that player lives up to the responsibilities of being a team member. Responsible coaches, like responsible parents, take advantage of moral dilemmas to promote character development among their players.

For example, in a soccer scrimmage where the score is tied, time is running out, and one team must first get the ball in order to have a chance of winning, the coach might stop the activity, sit the teams down and present the dilemma: Is it okay to intentionally foul your opponent or fake an injury in order to have a time-out called? The responses, both for and against intentional fouling and faking injury, will allow the coach to promote moral reasoning and moral growth.

Athletes who are positively socialized act responsibly, are concerned about others, and work cooperatively toward achieving common goals. To do this they need to have positive attitudes, moral reasoning, and self-discipline.

Guidelines for Developing Character

- *Clearly explain appropriate and inappropriate behaviors*
- *Explain and enforce penalties for violating appropriate behaviors*
- *Use role models to reinforce desired behaviors*
- *Use "teachable moments" to emphasize positive character traits*

Positive Attitudes

A major function of character development is to transfer the attitudes and values of our culture from one generation to the next. Attitudes are learned. They are based on knowledge or ignorance, and may be positive or negative. They lead to judgements about something or someone.

Character reflects the values that we hold and is an outgrowth of attitudes. For example, children who do not like vigorous physical activity and try to avoid it are frequently accused of being lazy or having bad attitudes. For whatever reason, they have developed negative attitudes toward vigorous activity. As a result, they will go to great lengths to avoid being physically active.

Attitudes toward activities, places, events, and people are learned behaviors acquired in social settings. As a result, they may be shaped, modified, or changed. To acquire an attitude that results in personal meaning, three things must occur: compliance, identification, and internalization.

Sportsmanship

The combined result of fair play, teamwork, loyalty, and self-control in both victory and defeat.

- *Fair Play: To play according to the rules and to apply them equally to all.*
- *Teamwork: To work cooperatively with one or more persons toward a common goal.*
- *Loyalty: To be consistent and faithful to an individual, group, or team.*
- *Self-control: To be in control of and responsible for one's actions.*

Compliance means doing something to get a favorable response from someone else. For example, a child may share his soccer ball with a playmate in the hope of getting a favorable response from the coach.

Identification, on the other hand, is a process that requires one to adopt the attitude of another person. In the example, the child now shares his soccer ball with a teammate because he knows that is what the coach would do.

Internalization means taking on a particular behavior as part of one's own value system. The child now shares his soccer ball because he wants to. The child has finally internalized the positive character trait of sharing.

Youth sport programs have both the opportunity and the responsibility to shape positive attitudes and help players value participation in vigorous physical activity. Sport also helps children internalize standards of proper behavior and conduct such as honesty, tolerance, acceptance, and empathy. As a parent, look for mature coaches who reinforce the values you instill at home.

Moral Reasoning and Behavior

Children have both the potential and the need for higher levels of moral behavior. *Moral reasoning* involves making intelligent decisions about what is right and wrong. *Moral behavior* is the ability to operate consistently within a value system that has reasoned right from wrong. Sport has the potential to foster real moral growth in the emotional and unpredictable situations that arise. Refraining from lying, cheating, and intimidating opponents are moral decisions governed by concern for the welfare of others.

A moral dilemma is a situation, real or manufactured, that offers an opportunity for moral reasoning and moral decision making. When these dilemmas arise, the coach has an excellent opportunity to call attention to them, helping players sort through what is good, right, and fair.

Moral questioning involves distinguishing between good and bad, right and wrong, or fair

---

Steps Leading to Moral Growth in Young Players

- *Create or take advantage of an existing moral dilemma. (For example, discuss player cheating in self-reporting scores.)*
- *Ask those involved to describe the dilemma. ("What happened?" "Why did it happen?" "How did it happen?")*
- *Help players focus on the specific word or term describing the dilemma. ("This is an issue involving _____." The word might be honesty, fair play, communication, cooperation, teamwork, or sportsmanship.)*
- *Work with players to define the meaning of the word and its consequences if ignored. ("Honesty is being truthful, trustworthy, and fair. Failure to be honest leads to, or results in _____.")*
- *Generalize the meaning of the word and its importance to the current situation. ("Why is it important to be honest when recording scores?")*
- *Apply the concept implied by the word first to other topics in the same setting and then to other areas. ("What are other areas in sports where honesty is very important?" followed by: "Why is honesty important in all that we do?")*
- *Reinforce positive moral behaviors whenever possible. ("I'm sure pleased with the accurate and honest reporting of your scores.")*

---

and unfair. If questioning doesn't occur, it is unlikely that moral reasoning, decision-making, and growth will result. Take time to discuss with your child situations that come up in his or her sport experiences that bring about moral questioning. They will allow you to reinforce some of life's most important lessons.

Self-Discipline

Self-discipline is the mental toughness and tenacity that we see in successful athletes. It is the realization that real effort, hard work, and personal sacrifice are necessary ingredients for success in sport and in life. Sport teaches that through self-discipline one can be successful.

As a parent you need to help your young player learn about self-discipline. You can do this by helping her get to practice on time, uphold team rules, and follow through on practice and game commitments. Praise her for dedicated, hard work.

With new players there is often the temptation to quit after the novelty of the sport and the glamour of being on a team wears off. Encouraging your player to honor her commitment for a specified amount of time. If she wants to quit at the end of the season, or after a pre-agreed length of time, okay. But help her to stick it out.

Tips for Motivating Young Players

- *Identify reasons for participating*
- *Help players select individual and team goals*
- *Help players improve old skills and learn new skills*
- *Make sport a fun and exciting process*
- *Reduce the stress of competition*
- *Help players gain a proper perspective on success*

Being Courageous

Courage is *not* the absence of fear. Being courageous is having the mental toughness to persevere in spite of fear. Courage comes in two forms: outer and inner. Outer or physical courage is built and tested when young players pit their skills against opponents and confront the fear of failure. It is also tested when they risk injury through their participation.

For example, in soccer young players outwardly display physical courage when dribbling down field against an opponent or marking an opponent. By helping players see competition as a personal challenge to build physical courage, coaches teach important lessons.

Inner courage is personal honesty, and overcoming the fear of looking foolish. Inner courage is found in players who distinguish right from wrong and act on the courage of their convictions. It is also found in players standing by commitments to their sport. Players with inner courage dare to do the right thing in spite of personal convenience or peer pressure. The inner courage is evident when a player commits to the hard work of team practice, constantly improves fitness and skill levels, and adheres to team training rules.

CONCEPT LEARNING

Sport participation is an active learning process closely related to mental development. Sport skill learning cannot occur without the benefit of higher thought processes. Concept learning is a process by which information is organized, put into memory, and made available for recall and application to a variety of settings.

Concept learning is an important outcome of youth sports. Concept learning provides players with the tools to use in decision making and application of skill concepts, movement concepts, activity concepts, and fitness concepts.

Concept Learning Through Sport

- **Skill Concepts:** *"How the body should move"*
  —*Fundamental skills, specialized skills*
- **Movement Concepts:** *"How my body can move"*
  —*Effort, space, relationships*
- **Fitness Concepts:** *"How my body functions"*
  —*Exercise frequency, exercise intensity, exercise time, exercise type*
- **Activity Concepts:** *"Where my body should move"*
  —*Rules, strategies, patterns, formations*

Skill Concepts

Skill concept learning deals specifically with how the body *should* move. Problems associated with insufficient instructional time, large groups, immaturity, or task complexity frequently make it difficult to develop skilled players within the confines of practice sessions. Therefore, young athletes must learn how their bodies are supposed to move to perform the various movement skills.

For example, a child may be unable to kick, dribble, or pass a ball. Unfortunately, the instructional portion of a practice session may be insufficient to help him become skillful. Similarly, older players often have trouble mastering complex strategies presented during practice. If, however, players are provided with the vital skill concepts about how their bodies should move when kicking, dribbling, and passing a ball, or performing specific plays, they have the necessary tools to learn outside regular practice.

As a parent, encourage your young athlete simply by helping her practice. Kicking, dribbling, and passing a soccer ball in the backyard is an excellent way to help your young player master the fundamental skills of the game.

Movement Concepts

Movement concept learning deals with how the body *can* move. Seldom does movement occur under the same conditions time after time. Most movement tasks in sport are fluid, which means players must be flexible. Changes in the playing surface, facilities, equipment, and number of participants make it impossible to address all the possibilities. When possible, spend some time with your child playing mini-games of one-on-one or two-on-two soccer, incorporating several of the kicking, dribbling and passing skills.

A new movement skill should first be practiced under controlled conditions, especially for novice players. Movement concept learning teaches players about the varied ways in which the body is capable of moving in performing a single skill or a group of sequential skills. Players need to be adaptable so they can move with control and efficiency under a variety of circumstances. You can help by playing with your child.

Activity Concepts

Activity concept learning deals with *where* the body should move. Activity concepts center on the learning of patterns, formations, rules, and strategies for effective participation in the sport. The activity concepts provide players with the essential knowledge of where they should position themselves, how to respond to elements of the game, and how to follow the rules and strategies for successful participation.

Activity concepts must be geared to the player's level of motor, cognitive, and social development. You can help by taking time with your child to understand such basic activity concepts as knowing the difference between offense and defense, learning the basic rules of the game, playing your position, anticipating an opponent's move, and listening to the official.

Fitness Concepts

Fitness concept learning deals with *what* one needs to do to gain and maintain a healthy lifestyle. Fitness enhancement is a laudable but elusive goal in programs that do not provide sufficient frequency, intensity, and time for conditioning effects to occur. Players must, however, learn fitness concepts for healthful living and be shown how they can incorporate these concepts into their daily lives. Seven-and eight-year-olds can begin to learn and apply basic anatomical terms such as *abdominal, biceps,* and *triceps* and physiological terms such as *target heart rate, aerobics,* and *static stretching.* They should also begin learning about the link between proper nutrition, fitness, and good health.

Mental Map Making

As movement skills are learned, mental maps or images are formed. These images are retained in memory, ready to be recalled and recreated instantly. As skill improves, performance appears almost automatic, with little or no conscious thought involved. Although movement skill performance is not truly automatic, the skill becomes so thoroughly learned that it appears to be.

For example, when your child walks he gives little attention to how, when, and exactly where he places one foot in front of the other.

He does not consciously think about how his arms swing in opposition to his leg action, or that he is striding forward in an alternating heel-to-toe fashion. These processes have been so thoroughly learned that they appear to be automatic because they do not require his conscious attention. If he tries, however, to walk on ice, in sand, or with a heavy backpack, the different set of conditions will cause him, for a short while, to think about and modify the requirements of the task until a new mental map has been formed and put into memory.

Strategies for Encouraging Young Players to Think Critically

- *Create a practice environment that requires players to think*
- *Be certain that the learning environment is supportive*
- *Use problem-solving techniques in each practice session*
- *Encourage players to ask why*
- *Help players learn how to form and test their own hypothesis*
- *Present game situations to players for discussion and reflection*
- *Encourage players to assist and give advice to one another*
- *Encourage players to problem solve in small groups*
- *Summarize sessions with challenges for out-of-practice problem solving*

2
Youth-Centered Sport

Youth-centered sport puts kids first. Youth-centered programs focus on learning the essential skills, rules and strategies of the sport, improving fitness levels, and having fun in the process.

AGE-GROUPING

Age-grouping in youth sport is a time honored tradition. The intent is to use your child's chronological age to match her for competition with others of similar physical, mental, emotional and social maturity levels. Although helpful, grouping players solely by grade level or age cannot determine your child's potential for success. The rate and level of sport skill learning is an individual process that depends on a combination of hereditary and environmental factors, as well as the complexity of the tasks.

If age-grouping is the standard means for equating kids for sport in your area, look for programs that group kids in increments of 2 years or less. In this way you can be reasonably assured that your 8-year-old will be placed appropriately in the 8-9 category with others at the same approximate level of ability. Putting an 8-year-old in an 8-12 category is comparable to placing midgets with giants.

If your child's skill levels exceed those of his peers, and he is not challenged in his age group, ask if he can be bumped into the next higher category. Make sure his playing time does not diminish.

Individualizing for Success

Individualizing for success is a good sign that the coach realizes that each player has a unique timetable for growth and development. Look for youth-centered programs that are geared to his phase of *sport skill development* (fundamental or specialized) and level of *sport skill learning* (novice, practice, or elite). Additionally, look for the inclusion of specific skill drills and training programs based on personal levels of *physical fitness* (both health fitness and skill fitness).

SPORT SKILL DEVELOPMENT

Skill development is the process of becoming competent in the performance of a wide vari-

---

Basics of Movement Skill Learning
Movement skill learning is a process that:

- *Progresses from simple to complex*
- *Moves from fundamental to specialized skills*
- *Is sequential and orderly in nature*
- *Varies in the rate of acquisition from player to player*
- *Builds skill upon skill*
- *Requires proficiency in the necessary fundamental skills prior to combining, refining, and utilizing them as sport skills*
- *Requires ample opportunities for practice, encouragement, and instruction*

ety of fundamental and specialized movement skills. Fundamental or basic skills should be mastered first so that specialized or sport skills can be learned, enabling players to perform with both competence and confidence in their abilities.

Fundamental Skills

Fundamental skills are the basic building blocks for success in sport. For example, running and jumping, kicking and receiving, leaping and dodging are important soccer fundamentals. Rolling, bending, twisting, springing, and balancing are critical gymnastics fundamentals.

Failure to master the basic skills of a sport early on only leads to frustration when a child attempts specialized skills. When players fail to learn the fundamental skills of the sport, they frequently pick up bad habits. It is much more difficult to unlearn faulty skills than to learn to do them correctly in the first place.

If you are really interested in maximizing the potential for success and enjoyment, help your child master the fundamentals before tackling the specialized skills of the game.

The period ranging from about 2 to 8 is generally considered to be the fundamental phase of development. This young age is an ideal time for your child to master the basics of many sports. Fundamental skills develop along a continuum of stages progressing from the initial to the elementary and finally to the mature stage.

The Initial Stage. At the initial stage of fundamental skill development your child will make the first observable and purposeful attempts at performing a task. This stage is characterized by relatively crude, uncoordinated movements. For example, your child may make valid attempts at running, jumping, kicking and receiving, but major components of the mature pattern are missing. Movements are either grossly exaggerated or inhibited. Rhythmically coordinated performance of the movement is also absent.

The Elementary Stage. The elementary stage is a transitional time between the initial and mature stages. Coordination and rhythmical performance improve, and your child gains

---

Soccer Skill Learning A Sequential Process:

Fundamental Soccer Skills:
- *Twisting/Turning*
- *Jumping*
- *Bending/Stretching*
- *Leaping*
- *Dodging/Feinting*
- *Kicking*
- *Running*
- *Stopping*

Specialized Soccer Skills:
- *Dribbling*
- *Juggling*
- *Passing*
- *Offensive Play*
- *Receiving*
- *Defensive Play*
- *Heading*
- *Goal Tending*
- *Marking*

---

greater control over movements. However, movements at this stage still appear somewhat awkward and lacking in coordination.

MASTERING FUNDAMENTAL SKILLS
Many children are at an immature stage in several fundamental skills because of insufficient practice, limited amounts of encouragement, and lack of proper instruction. They have failed to reach the mature stage necessary for success at the sport skill level. Youth-centered soccer focuses on helping young players progress to the mature stage in a wide variety of fundamental skills before introducing them to the more specialized skills of the game.

The Mature Stage. At the mature stage of fundamental skill development, all the component parts of a movement skill are put together into a well-coordinated and efficient performance. From here, performance improves rapidly. Young players are able to run faster, jump higher, and kick with greater accuracy after the mature stage has been attained. Mature fundamental skills may be continually refined, combined with other skills, and utilized in a variety of specialized sport activities.

Most children have the potential to reach the mature fundamental stage in many basic skills by age 6 or 7. Your young athlete may, however, reach this stage somewhat ahead or behind his peers. Remember, mature fundamental skills are the essential building blocks for the specialized skills of any sport.

Specialized Soccer Skills

Specialized sport skills are nothing more than basic skills that have been combined with other basic skills, and are more highly refined. As players improve, fundamental skills become more specialized and are used with greater precision and control.

Running, leaping, and jumping may be used in specific offense and defense strategies in soccer, basketball, gymnastics, and track. Basic kicking and ball control skills are used in a variety of dribbling, passing, goal shooting, and receiving skills in soccer. The fundamental skills of twisting and turning the body are applied to specific blocking and tackling techniques.

Youth-centered coaching recognizes the need to focus on the process aspects of skill learning before the product aspects. Look for a coach who expects players to master technique before they work on speed, distance, and accuracy.

The specialized skill phase of sport skill development typically begins around age 7 or 8. Most children begin to develop a keen interest in sport at about this time. They are eager to learn new skills and try them out in a wide variety of sports. Although it begins in childhood, sport skill learning frequently continues through adolescence and well into adulthood.

The Stages of Movement Skill Development

Fundamental Stages	Specialized Stages
Initial	*Transition*
Elementary	*Application*
Mature	*Lifelong Utilization*

The specialized phase of sport skill development can be subdivided into three stages—transition, application, and lifelong utilization.

The Transition Stage. The transition stage of specialized skill development generally begins around age 7 or 8 and extends to about age 10. Children at this stage usually express a high degree of interest in many sports, but possess little actual ability in any. If they have not developed mature fundamentals, they will be hampered in developing the specialized skills of the sport.

Give your young athlete opportunities during the transition stage to keep refining his fundamental skills, and to use them as sport skills in a variety of team, individual, and dual activities. For example, at the transition stage the fundamental skill of kicking is applied to the sport skill of using the instep kick in soccer. The instep kick can be practiced in exercise situations and then applied to a lead-up activity such as line soccer, circle soccer, or six-on-a-side soccer. At the transition stage the focus is not on playing the official sport, but rather on mastering the sport skills, general rules, and basic strategies of the game.

SPORT SPECIALIZATION
Sport specialization too early is unwise and inappropriate for most children. By providing children with opportunities to sharpen their skills and to pursue interests in a wide variety of sports, you are giving them the tools for making personally appropriate choices for a lifetime of healthful physical activity.

The Application Stage. Players at the application stage have begun to prefer certain sports, based primarily on previously successful experiences, body type, geographical location, and emotional, social, and cultural factors. The narrowing of interests is accompanied by an increased desire for competence. Form, precision, accuracy, and standards of good performance are all especially important to the learner at the application stage. Therefore, more complex skills are practiced, and strategies and rules take on greater importance.

The application stage is typical of middle and junior high school students, from about 11 to 13 years of age. However, with the surge of participation throughout North America in youth sport programs, this stage may actually begin much earlier. Many soccer players apply their movement skills to organized sports participation by age 6 or even sooner. The key element at the application stage is that players have developed sufficient skills and knowledge of the game to use meaningfully in competitive or recreational settings.

The Lifelong Utilization Stage. The lifelong utilization stage is based on previous sport and fundamental skill stages and continues throughout life. At this stage, high interest in specific activities is evidenced through regular participation. The game of soccer may be selected as a lifetime activity for fun, fitness, and competitive fulfillment on an organized or recreational basis.

Factors Affecting Sport Skill Development

A variety of factors play an important role in soccer skill development. Players need frequent opportunities for practice, positive encouragement, quality instruction, and healthful learning environments. Childhood is recognized as a critical period for mastering fundamental movement skills. Simply getting older or bigger will not cause soccer skill mastery. Players who have mastered the fundamentals of the game are ready to begin the exciting process of specialized skill learning and testing their skills out in healthy forms of competitive and recreational play.

Types of Sport Skills

Soccer skills may be classified as *fixed skills* and *fluid skills*. As a general rule it is best to introduce new skills (novice level) under fixed conditions and work progressively to more fluid conditions. The basic differences between fixed and fluid are time, space, pressure, and decision making.

Fluid Skills. Fluid skills are responses to a constantly changing and unpredictable environment. Bringing a soccer ball up field against a defensive player involves skills performed in a constantly changing environment. Rapid and

---

Fixed and Fluid Sport Skills
Youth coaches need to:

- *Identify type of activity (i.e., fixed or fluid)*
- *Set up practice sessions consistent with the fluid or fixed nature of activities*
- *Introduce fluid activities under fixed conditions first (i.e., control the environment and conditions of skill practice initially)*
- *Introduce situations that require responses to sudden and unpredictable cues in fluid activities as skill develops*
- *Strive for greater consistency, duplication, and reducing environmental cues for fixed activities as skill develops*
- *Encourage players to "think through" the activity in early stages of learning only*
- *Encourage players to "screen" out unnecessary cues as skill develops*

---

flexible decision making are required. Coaches need to recognize the nature of dynamic activities and provide opportunities that promote rapid decision making and adaptive behaviors in a variety of game-like situations.

Fixed Skills. Fixed skills require performance under a given set of conditions. The player is permitted to move at his own pace through the activity and has time to recognize and respond to the specific conditions of the environment. Fixed skills generally emphasize accuracy, consistency, or repetition of performance.

LEARNING FLUID AND FIXED SKILLS
As a general rule new skills should be introduced under fixed conditions. Players have a chance to focus on one skill at a time and increase their chances for success. As the skill develops it is then practiced under fluid conditions in which the environmental conditions are flexible and constantly changing. Soccer dribbling and passing, for example, are best learned under fixed conditions. Once the basics have been mastered they need to be practiced under increasingly fluid conditions.

Learning New Skills

Soccer skill learning, whether performed under fixed or fluid conditions, occurs in a sequence that may be classified into broad levels: novice, practice, and elite. Each level refers to a period during which both the learner and the coach have specific identifiable tasks and responsibilities. In the real world players will be at many different levels of soccer skill development on the same team, because the new skill learning is age-independent. Both younger and older players go through the same sequence when learning a new skill.

The words in parenthesis are the terms most widely used and accepted when discussing a soccer teaching progression and skill aquisition.

The Novice Level
Youth coaches provide players with the general idea of the skill.

- *Introduce the major aspects of the skill only (be brief)*
- *Demonstrate the skill*
- *Permit players to try out the skill*
- *Provide plenty of opportunity for exploring the skill itself and self-discovery of its general principles*
- *Compare the new skill, when possible, to a similar skill that players may be familiar with*
- *Provide immediate, precise, and positive encouragement concerning the skill*
- *Focus on the process (i.e., form) not the product (i.e., how far, how fast)*

The Novice Level (Fundamental). At the novice level, movements of players are generally uncoordinated. The learner begins to construct mental pictures of the skills and actively tries to understand them. Because of the conscious attention given to every detail of the tasks themselves, performance is poor. Players often experience fatigue early in the activity, caused more by the mental requirements of the tasks than by the performance. At this level players tend to pay attention to all the information that is available, but are unable to screen out what is not important.

Coaches of novices need to be aware of the conscious thinking requirements and understand that the goal during this period should be only to help players get a general idea of how to perform the essential skills of the game.

The Practice Level
Youth coaches focus on practice conditions to promote skill refinement.

- *Provide lots of opportunities for practice*
- *Work on skill refinement in a supportive non-threatening environment*
- *Devise practice situations that progressively focus on skill refinement*
- *Make practice sessions short and fast paced with frequent short breaks prior to longer sessions with fewer breaks*
- *Analyze skill and provide players with helpful encouragement*
- *Structure quality practice sessions that focus on quality performance Remember: "perfect practice makes perfect"*
- *Provide frequent, precise, immediate, and positive encouragement*
- *Allow for individual differences in the rate of skill learning*
- *Focus attention on the whole skill whenever possible*
- *Practice at the rate and in the manner that the skill will be used during competitive performance of the activity*

The Practice Level (Game/Match Related). The practice level begins after players understand the skills in general and are able to perform them in a manner close to the final product. The skills at this level serve a real purpose and are practiced over and over. Conscious attention to their smaller parts decreases. Players begin to devote more attention to the goal or product of the skills than to the process itself. The poorly coordinated, jerky movements so evident at the novice level gradually disappear.

Players begin to get a "feel" for the skills as their kinesthetic sensitivities become more highly attuned. They rely less on verbal and visual cues and more on muscle sense.

Coaches of players at the practice level recognize that their athletes understand the skills. They set up practice sessions that focus on refining skills and maximizing performer feedback under a variety of simulated performance conditions.

The Elite Level
Youth coaches focus on further refinement, skill maintenance, and encouragement.

- *Structure practice opportunities that promote intensity and enthusiasm*
- *Provide encouragement, motivation, and positive support*
- *Offer suggestions and tips on strategy*
- *Structure practices that duplicate game-like situations*
- *Help players anticipate their actions in game-like situations*
- *Know players as individuals and adjust methods to meet their needs*
- *Provide encouragement that focuses on specific aspects of the skill*
- *Avoid requiring players to think about execution of the skill: This can cause "analysis paralysis"*

The Elite Level (Game/Match Conditions). Players at the elite level have a complete understanding of the skills essential for success. Mental plans are highly developed, and players need to pay very little attention to the conscious thinking aspects of performing a skill. Performers at the elite level are able to ignore unnecessary information and are not bothered by distractions. They have excellent timing and anticipation of movements.

In youth soccer only a few players reach the elite level. Most are at the novice and practice levels. Coaches of young soccer players at the elite level should focus on further refining and maintaining skills and on providing selected feedback.

Cues for Correcting or Refining a Well-Learned Technique
Youth coaches are often called upon to change well-learned but incorrectly performed skills.

- *Determine if there is enough time to make the change (think in terms of weeks and months, not hours or days)*
- *Determine if the player really wants to make the change*
- *Be certain that the player understands why the change is being made*
- *Be certain that the player realizes that performance will generally get poorer before it gets better*
- *Provide a supportive, encouraging environment*
- *Structure practice sessions that gradually bring the player from the novice to the practice and finally to the elite level*

Practice With Parents

All too frequently coaches have too many players and too little time. Soccer skill learning takes time, and "practice with parents" is a partial answer to this dilemma. By giving players tasks to work on at home, coaches utilize your help (and that of grandparents and older siblings).

Practice with Parents

- *Use encouragement prior to and immediately following performance*
- *Tell the player the cause of any error (be precise)*
- *Tell the player how to correct any error (be concise)*
- *Check to see that the player understands the information given*
- *Focus on correcting one error at a time*
- *Use positive reinforcement techniques*
- *Reward approximations*
- *Encourage players to improve through self-practice*
- *Provide ample opportunities for knowledge of results*
- *Encourage skill analysis during the novice and practice levels of skill learning*

Individual take-home sheets contain essential fundamentals of the game and practice activities to encourage further participation. They guide adults in what to do and how to do it. Take home sheets provide visual and verbal information about the key elements of fundamental and specialized skills to practice, and are excellent motivators for young players.

FITNESS ENHANCEMENT

Improved physical fitness is an important outcome of participation in youth sport. Basically, physical fitness is a positive state of well-being influenced by regular, vigorous physical activity, genetic makeup, and nutritional adequacy.

The health status of players suggests the upper and lower limits of fitness that can be reasonably expected. Nutritional status greatly enhances or inhibits players' energy level, and genetic structure limits the ultimate level of fitness attainable. All three factors should be considered in the development and maintenance of your player's health or skill fitness.

Muscular strength, muscular endurance, cardiovascular endurance, joint flexibility, and body composition are generally considered to be health fitness components. Balance, coordination, agility, speed, and power are the primary components of skill fitness.

Health Fitness

Health fitness is a relative state of being, not an ability, skill, or capacity. Health fitness can be readily improved through any regular vigorous physical activity, or decreased through inactivity and disuse. Young soccer players should strive for and maintain personal standards of health fitness.

Elements of Health Fitness

- *Muscular Strength*
- *Muscular Endurance*
- *Cardiovascular Endurance*
- *Joint Flexibility*
- *Body Composition*

Muscular Strength. Muscular strength is the maximum force that can be exerted by a group of muscles. Muscular strength is determined by the size of the muscle, its chemical composition, and nerve impulses to the muscle fibers. Participation in a youth soccer program does much to improve leg strength.

Muscular Endurance. Muscular endurance is the ability to perform repeated muscle contractions without being limited by fatigue. Muscular endurance is similar to muscular strength in terms of the activities performed but differs in emphasis. Endurance-building activities require less overload on the muscles but require a greater number of repetitions. Players performing several sit-ups, pull-ups, or push-ups are performing muscular endurance activities.

Cardiovascular Endurance. Cardiovascular endurance is specific to the heart, lungs, and vascular systems. It is the single most important aspect of physical fitness. Cardiovascular endurance is the ability to perform sustained repetitions of an activity requiring considerable use of the circulatory and respiratory systems. Cardiovascular endurance is dependent, in large part, on the lifestyle of the individual player. The keys to developing cardiovascular endurance are exercise frequency, exercise duration, and exercise intensity. The greater the frequency, the longer the duration, the more intense the workout, the greater the improvement of the player's cardiovascular endurance.

Joint Flexibility. Joint flexibility is the ability of the various joints of the body to move through their full ranges of motion. Flexibility is joint-specific and can be improved with practice. The constant bending, twisting, turning, and stretching required of most sports, along with the natural elasticity of young bodies, account for much of the flexibility seen in young athletes. All too often, however, range of motion rapidly decreases with age because of lack of activity.

Body Composition. Body composition is the proportion of lean body mass to fat body mass. Body composition is an important aspect of overall health and fitness. Being *over fat* is the issue, not being *overweight*, as determined by traditional height-weight tables. The calorie burning benefits of soccer play an important role in helping players achieve their ideal body compositions.

Skill Fitness

The development and maintenance of skill fitness is a function of practice and skill development, within broadly defined genetic limits. Balance, coordination, agility, speed, and power are the most frequently cited components of skill fitness.

Balance. Balance is a complex aspect of skill fitness influenced by vision, the inner ear, the brain, nerve endings in muscles, joints and tendons, and the skeletal muscles. Balance is the ability to maintain one's equilibrium in relation to the force of gravity and to make minute alterations in one's body position when it is placed in various positions. Balance is critically important in soccer and may be divided into static and dynamic balance components.

Static balance is the ability to maintain balance in a fixed position, such as when standing on one foot. Adequate static balance ability is an essential building block for the important dynamic balance skills of soccer.

Dynamic balance is the ability to maintain equilibrium while the body is in motion, when dribbling the ball down field, jumping in or marking an opponent.

In actuality, all movement involves elements of both static and dynamic balance.

Coordination. Coordination is the ability to put both motor and sensory systems, usually vision, together into efficient movement. Various parts of the body may be involved, such as eye-foot coordination when kicking a soccer ball or passing it to a teammate. Eye-hand coordination is seen in the goalkeeper's quick responses, and eye-body coordination is efficient in ball juggling skills.

Agility. Agility is the ability to change direction of the entire body quickly without loss of balance or sense of body position. Agility, sometimes referred to as "quickness," is a combination of strength, speed, coordination, and power. This ability may be enhanced in young players through participation in soccer skill drills that involve ball control and dodging activities. Offensive players attacking through a maze of defenders need great agility.

Speed. Speed is the ability to move the body or any of its parts quickly. Speed is directly related to muscle power, and is essential for young soccer players as they run, jump, and leap, or when they kick the ball. A player's speed is influenced by the combination of both reaction time and movement time.

Reaction time is the amount of time from the brain's signal "go" to the first movement of the body. Good reaction time helps a player anticipate and respond to game situations rapidly.

Movement time is the time from the player's first movement to completion of the activity. Good movement time helps a player get from point to point in the shortest time possible.

Power. Power is a player's ability to perform one maximum explosive effort in as short a period as possible. Power combines elements of strength and speed. It's an important aspect of most sports and is seen in soccer in running, leaping, jumping and kicking for maximum speed and distance.

Exercise Thresholds

A player's threshold of training is the minimum amount of exercise required to produce fitness gains. Young athletes new to a fitness training program can begin at or near their threshold levels and gradually increase their activity in terms of exercise frequency, intensity, time, and type (FIT). The goal, therefore, is to gradually increase these three components until the target zone is reached. The *target zone* is the point at which maximum benefits are obtained for a player's individual level of fitness.

Fitness Fun For Everyone

The reality of making measurable contributions to the fitness levels of young players is frequently quite limited. Insufficient time to attain a training effect from vigorous physical activity is the single greatest deterrent to the young athlete's fitness enhancement. Coaches may assign "fitness fun for everyone" as an extension of the practice period.

Fitness fun may take many forms. Players may simply be assigned fitness tasks to complete during commercial breaks of their television watching time. Later they may be asked to informally report to parents and coaches on their progress and frequency of compliance. Fitness fun may also take the form of a home fitness chart sent to parents with an explanation of various fitness activities, their purpose, and supervisory hints.

The athletic experience goes beyond fitness "training" and recognizes the importance of fitness "education." Fitness training can occur with little or no enthusiasm or comprehension of why it is important, or how to go about it. Fitness education, on the other hand, recognizes that it is vitally important for players to know **why** fitness enhancement is personally important, to know **how** to go about it in a safe and healthful manner, and to be sufficiently **motivated** to participate with little or no outside prodding.

American boys and girls are less fit than their counterparts of 10, 20, or even 30 years ago. The popular belief that they get plenty of regular, vigorous physical activity as a normal part of their everyday routines is no more than a myth for millions. This disgraceful situation can be eliminated if we help kids improve their movement skills and make improvement of youth fitness a national priority.

Just look at the many positive benefits of vigorous physical activity:

Increased Muscular Strength and Endurance

- Stimulates bone growth
- Increases bone mineralization
- Reduces susceptibility to injury
- Enhances self-concept
- Improves body image
- Aids in physical appearance

Improved Levels of Cardiovascular Endurance

- Improves lung capacity
- Strengthens the heart muscle
- Improves circulation
- Reduces cholesterol levels (LDL)
- Lowers heart rate
- Increases oxygen carrying capacity (VO2 max)

- Aids in stress reduction
- Promotes relaxation
- May reduce susceptibility to the common cold

Greater Joint Flexibility

- Promotes injury prevention
- Increases work/play efficiency
- Improves motor performance
- Increases range of motion
- Promotes fluidity of movement

Individually Optimum Body Composition

- Improves circulatory efficiency

- Reduces respiratory distress
- Reduces susceptibility to some diseases
- Enhances self-concept

Improved Skill Fitness

- Improves sport performance
- Aids in weight control
- Provides the tools for enhancing health-related fitness
- Promotes injury reduction
- Encourages regular active participation

3
The Effective Teacher/Coach

The youth soccer coach is called on to fill many roles, but none is more important than that of being a good teacher. **Good teaching is the foundation for successful coaching.**

To be an effective teacher a coach must:

- Clearly communicate what is to be learned
- Evaluate the athletes' abilities
- Use a coaching style that fits the needs of young athletes
- Be consistent and systematic in teaching
- Alter lesson plans and game strategies on the basis of how effectively objectives are being met

If you are a beginning or novice parent/ coach *don't* try to teach or coach too much. Facilitate the safety and organization of the practice and let the game be the teacher. Use the following chapter as a guideline to assist you.

GUIDELINES TO GOOD TEACHING

Although there are many ways to instruct young soccer players, the inexperienced coach will find the following sequence easy to use and effective in teaching and refining skills.

Young players learn best by participating. They do not learn well by sitting and listening to coaches lecture. **A good rule is, "When I speak, I want you to stop what you're doing and listen."** Do not violate your own rule by continuing to talk when players are not paying attention.

Prior to your instruction:

- be sure you have the attention of all players

- tell them precisely what you want them to learn; do this in one minute or less, preferably with a physical demonstration of the skill
- have players practice the skill while you observe them and provide feedback
- have players come back to a group setting and discuss the adjustments that are needed for improvement (if necessary)
- place the players into groups by ability; continue to practice and provide feedback
- repeat the last two steps as frequently as needed until the desired level of competence is achieved.

The following steps to good teaching are effective in a variety of settings, including the teaching of young athletes.

Be Realistic

Players will respond to realistic and challenging expectations. Conversely, expectations that are beyond their achievement will decrease the motivation of even the most skillful players. Set short-term goals on an individual basis and adjust them when they are achieved.

Structure Instruction

Every practice must have well-defined objectives and a systematic plan of instruction. The critical steps to a structured lesson are:

- select the essential skills, rules, and strategies from the many options available
- clearly identify elements of acceptable performance for each skill

- organize and conduct your practices to maximize the opportunity your players have to acquire the skill(s)

Establish an Orderly Environment

State your clear expectations of what is to be accomplished at each practice. Players must be held accountable for being on time and coming to the practice ready to learn. Young players do not learn effectively in long, boring practices that involve drills that do not relate to their understanding of the game.

Maintain Consistent Discipline

Keeping control of your team is much easier than regaining control once problems with misbehavior have disrupted your authority. Prevent the types of misbehavior that arise when coaches do not anticipate and avoid problems with discipline.

Prevent Misbehavior: Although threats and lectures may prevent misbehavior in the short-term, their effectiveness is short-lived. Moreover, this type of relationship between a coach and team members does not promote learning the game of soccer, nor does it motivate the players to accept the coach's instructions.

Sound discipline involves two steps that must be in place before misbehavior occurs. They are:

- Define how players are to behave and identify misbehavior that will not be tolerated.
- Identify the consequences for individuals who do not behave according to the rules.

Children want clearly defined limits and structure for how they should behave. This can be accomplished without showing anger, lecturing, or threatening. As the coach, it is the coach's responsibility to have a systematic plan for maintaining discipline before your season gets underway.

Define Team Rules: Identify what you consider to be desirable and undesirable conduct by your players. This list can then be used to establish relevant team rules. A list of potential items to consider when identifying team rules is included.

Desirable and Undesirable Conduct in Soccer

Desirable Conduct
- *Attending to coach's instructions*
- *Full concentration on exercises*
- *Treating opponents with respect*
- *Giving positive encouragement to teammates*
- *Avoiding penalties*
- *Being prompt to practices and games*
- *Helping to pick up equipment after practices*
- *Bringing all equipment to practices*

Undesirable Conduct
- *Talking while instructions are being given*
- *Inattentive behavior during exercises*
- *Fighting with opponents or using abusive language*
- *Making negative comments about teammates*
- *Intentionally fouling during the game*
- *Being late or absent from practices and games*
- *Leaving equipment out for others to pick up*
- *Forgetting to bring equipment or uniform to games and practices*

Enforce Rules: Rules are enforced through rewards and penalties. **When determining rewards and penalties for rules, the most effective approach is to use rewards that are meaningful to your players and appropriate to the situation.** Withdrawal of rewards should be used for misconduct.

The best way to motivate players to behave in an acceptable manner is to reward them for good behavior.

Penalties are only effective when they are meaningful to the players. Examples of ineffective penalties include showing anger, embarrassing players by lecturing them in the presence of team members or adults, shouting at players, or assigning a physical activity (laps, extra pushups). Avoid using physical activity as a form of punishment; the benefits of soccer are gained through activity.

Children should not associate activity with punishment.

A more positive approach to handling misbehavior is to prevent it by establishing, with player input, clear team rules. Use fair and consistent enforcement of the rules, primarily through rewarding correct behavior, rather than penalizing unacceptable behavior.

Group Players According to Ability

Your soccer team will most likely have players at various levels of ability. For effective learning the players must often be divided into smaller groups. Organize players effectively so they are practicing at levels that will advance their playing abilities.

- When a new skill, rule, or strategy is being taught that all your athletes need to know, use a single group instructional setting.
- As you identify differences in ability, place players of similar ability in smaller groups.
- When practicing a skill, rule, or strategy for which individual athletes are at several levels (initial, intermediate, or later learning levels), establish learning stations that focus on specific outcomes.

Organize the groups so that there is a systematic order in which players take turns. Each group must know precisely what is to be learned. Supervise each group by rotating and spending short periods of time with each. Avoid spending all of the instructional time with one group. If any group is favored during small group instruction, it should be those players who are the least skillful.

Maximize Task Time

Progress in skill development is directly related to the amount of time that players spend practicing in game-like situations. Practices provide the opportunity to attempt a specific skill repeatedly under guided instruction. Coaches should conduct their practices to simulate game situations, while adjusting the environment to meet the developmental levels of the various athletes. **Practices are the most effective learning environment for perfecting physical and mental skills.**

- Plan and outline the practice. The planning phase of any practice is a key element in the success of that practice.
- Reduce the number of athletes who are waiting in line by using small groups in drills.
- Provide sufficient equipment so that players do not have to take turns to use it.
- Schedule your drills so that one leads into the next without major set-up time.
- Clearly outline and/or diagram each portion of practice and communicate as much of that information as possible before going on the field.
- Complete as many pre-and post-warmup/cool down activities as possible.
- Recruit aides (parents and older players) to help with instructional stations under your supervision.

Maximize Success Rates

Achieving a desired outcome is a strong motivator to continue. This relationship between **attempts** and *successes* mandates that coaches structure their practices so that players will succeed on a high proportion of their early attempts. The following hints have been used by successful youth soccer coaches:

- Reduce each skill, rule, or strategy into achievable sub-skills and focus instruction on those sub-skills.
- Provide feedback to the athlete so that, on most occasions, something that he did is rewarded, followed by specific instructions about what needs more work, ending with an encouraging, "Try again."

Monitor Progress

Players learn most effectively during practices that are accompanied by meaningful feedback. In youth soccer, the meaningful feedback is most frequently provided by the coach or assistant coaches. If left to their own agendas, young players may practice inappropriate skills or they may practice pertinent skills inappropriately. Coaches must conduct practices with the correct balance between feedback and independent learning.

EFFECTIVE PRACTICES

The keys to effective practices are **careful planning** and *sound instruction*. Both ingredients are under the control of the coach. Each practice should:

- be based upon previous planning, seasonal organization, needs of the team, and needs of the players
- list the objectives and key points that will be the focus of instruction for that practice
- show the amount of time allotted to each objective during the practice
- identify the activities (instructional, drill, or scrimmage) that will be used to teach or practice the objectives
- apply the guidelines for effective instruction included in this chapter
- include an evaluation of the strengths and weaknesses of the practice.

The amount of time that players can attend to a coach's instruction depends on their ages and developmental levels. Generally players aged 10 and under cannot effectively tolerate more than one hour of concentrated practice. As age and abilities advance, practices can be slightly longer. **Use the time that is available effectively.**

A common pitfall in youth soccer is to define far too many objectives and then teach for exposure rather than mastery. When insufficient time is devoted to important skills, the result is incompetence and frustration.

Distribute practice time across several objectives, then devote sufficient time to each objective so that a meaningful change in the performance of 80 percent of the players has occurred. Devote time in additional practices to the objective until the players are able to transfer the skill into game-like drills. At that point, they can be expected to transfer the skills of practice into their games.

Drills That Work

The two most important components of your practices are the **development of individual skills** and the translation of these **skills into game-like situations through drills.** The drills must be related to the team's objectives. Too often coaches use exercises that are traditional or favorites of the players but that have no relevance to the skills to be learned. Drills should be selected or developed according to the following features:

- have a meaningful objective
- require a relatively short explanation
- provide an excellent opportunity for players to master the skill or concept
- keep players "on task"
- be easily modified to accommodate skilled and unskilled players
- provide opportunity for skill analysis and feedback to players
- be challenging and fun

Write your exercises on single sheets or cards. After the practice, write your comments about the exercise's usefulness directly on the card and file the card for future use. Good exercises can be used many times during a season. Share your exercises with fellow coaches. Such activities promote fellowship among coaches and provide the beginning coach with a repertoire of useful teaching tools and techniques.

Protect the Safety of Players

In addition to providing effective instruction, the coach has the responsibility of ensuring that all practices and games are conducted in a safe environment (See Chapter 13). Therefore, the coach's primary responsibility can be summed up in this statement: **Teach for improved competence and safety every day.**

Legal experts have identified as many as 12, and as few as 5, legal competencies expected of coaches at any level of participation. All agree that the foundation of coaching competency is effective teaching. Coaches should consider 8 additional competencies:

- effective supervision
- effective reaction to medical emergencies
- providing safe equipment
- providing safe facilities
- safe transportation
- matching players according to size, skill, and maturity
- providing "Due Process"
- providing competent assistants

Coaches, in any sport, owe certain legal obligations to their players. The following identifies those legal obligations for coaches, then translates them into coaching conduct or behavior.

EFFECTIVE TEACHING

Legal Obligation: Coaches are supposed to be teachers first and foremost.

Coaching Behavior: Enroll in certification and continuing coaching education programs, and start your own reading education program in coaching and communication skills.

EFFECTIVE SUPERVISION

Legal Obligation: Coaches are responsible for team supervision wherever and whenever the team meets.

Coaching Behavior: Recruit competent assistants, and establish a plan of supervision for all team practices, meetings, games, and other events.

EFFECTIVE REACTION TO MEDICAL EMERGENCIES

Legal Obligation: Coaches are supposed to know medical emergencies when they see them, and to know how to respond quickly and responsibly.

Coaching Behavior: Take a certification course in emergency medical procedures, or at least first aid, and establish a plan for prompt reaction to medical emergencies.

PROVIDING SAFE EQUIPMENT

Legal Obligation: Coaches are supposed to know how to identify, fit, and maintain safe sports equipment.

Coaching Behavior: Establish equipment fitting, distribution, and maintenance plans in accordance with all manufacturer warranties, guidelines, and directions; take continuing education programs regarding equipment; maintain records on equipment inspection and reconditioning.

PROVIDING SAFE FACILITIES

Legal Obligation: Coaches are supposed to know when field or surface conditions pose a danger to players.

Coaching Behavior: Take continuing education programs regarding facility operations; establish a plan for regular inspections of field or surface inspections, including quick repair of defects or problems.

PROVIDING SAFE TRANSPORTATION

Legal Obligation: Coaches are supposed to know how players are being transported to away games or events, and with whom the players will be traveling.

Coaching Behavior: Use the league and parents to help establish transportation plans that include approved drivers, vehicles, and stops; establish a team code of travel conduct.

PROVIDING DUE PROCESS

Legal Obligation: Coaches have to establish fair rules and policies, and explain their reasons for suspending a player from the team.

Coaching Behavior: Use the league and parents to establish rules and policies regarding team conduct; provide written copies of rules and policies to players and their parents; never suspend a player without giving the player and his parents the chance to explain their conduct.

PROVIDING COMPETENT ASSISTANTS

Legal Obligation: Coaches are supposed to recruit or assign assistant coaches who are as competent as the head coach. Often it is the younger assistant coach that actually may have more practical soccer experience than the parent/coach who never played before.

Coaching Behavior: Start a training program just for the assistant coaches; plan and organize the staff with continuing education and training as a requirement.

Let The Game Teach. . . .

"One of the most common faults of youth coaches is stopping practice too often and over-coaching the players. An overall philosophy that is a good foundation for any coach is to facilitate small-sided games with various conditions that highlight different aspects of play and **let the game be the teacher.** *Children learn through self-discovery and experimentation. Maximize their practice time with playing soccer—not listening to the coach."*

Glenn Myernick, Coaching Coordinator United States Soccer

4
Soccer Rules of Play
(With Modifications for the Youth Game)

INTRODUCTION

The laws of the game are the official regulations established by the Federation Internationale De Football Association (FIFA). They govern play according to a uniform set of international standards.

According to FIFA, the types of modifications permissible for players of school age are limited to five specific areas: (a) the size of the field; (b) the size, weight, and material of the ball; (c) the width between the goal posts and the height of the cross bar from the ground; (d) the duration of the game; and (e) the number of substitutions that can be used in a game. This chapter contains statements and interpretations of the laws of play as well as suggested modifications for youth play.

Modifications in the laws for youth play are presented to maintain the principles and spirit of the laws of the game while meeting the educational and developmental needs of youth players. Modifications are included as a progression to:

- help coaches develop a systematic approach to teaching the game of soccer to their athletes
- help youth players to master the skills of soccer so they may ultimately play under the official laws of the game.

LAWS OF PLAY

Law I—The Field of Play

The soccer field must be rectangular. Each line, mark, or fixture has a specific purpose (Figure 4-1). These purposes include:

- to determine if a goal is scored
- to determine if the ball is in or out of play
- to identify important areas of the field
- to aid in the start and restart of play

Practical Considerations. The field must be safe and free of hazardous objects such as rocks, glass, and projecting structures (pipes and sewer covers). Goal nets and corner flags should be used.

Modifications for Youth Play. Field sizes for younger players (ages 6-11) should be smaller than the regulation field (Table 4-1). Large fields can be divided so that several teams can play at the same time (Figure 4-2).

Law II—The Ball

A spherical ball made of leather or approved synthetic materials, with a 27-to 28-inch circumference and a weight of 14 to 16 ounces, is to be used for play. This is a standard size 5 ball.

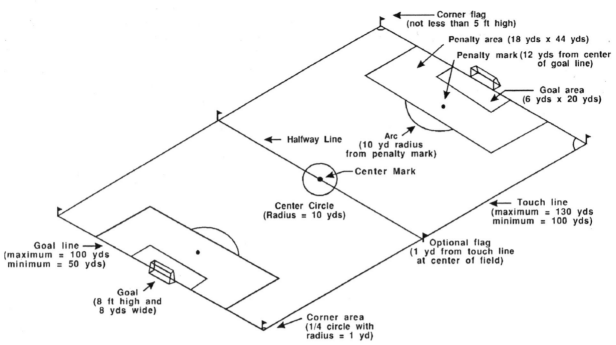

Figure 4-1. Regulation field of play.

Table 4-1. Recommended field for 11 players per side.

Age Group (Years)	Dimensions (in yards)	
	Width	Length
< 8	50	60–80
8–11	50–60	80–110
> 12	60–75	110–120

*Note that 11 per side games are not recommended for youth players below the age of 11 years. However, if a league tradition of full-sided games is difficult to alter, the above dimensions are recommended.

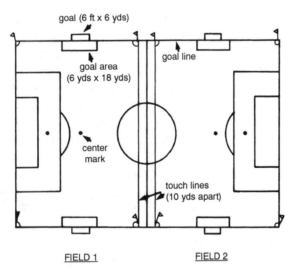

Figure 4-2. Two fields for small-sided games on a full-size soccer field.

Practical Consideration. Balls must be safe for play and properly inflated.

Modifications for Youth Play. Use of smaller and lighter balls permits younger players to kick, punt, and throw greater distances. However, smaller balls are more difficult to maneuver and accurately pass and shoot. Ball sizes commonly used for different age groups, with their corresponding dimensions, are presented in Table 4-2.

- Balls used for youth play should be compatible with the physical characteristics of young athletes.
- Balls that are too large (or small), heavy, or hard may discourage or hurt younger players.

Table 4-2. Ball sizes commonly used for play.

Age Group (Years)	Ball Size	Circumference (Inches)	Weight (Ounces)
< 8	3	23–25	10–12
8–11	4	25–27	12–14
> 12	5	27–28	14–16

Law III—Number of Players

Full-sided games are played by two teams of 11 players each. Games can be started as long as each team has at least seven players present. One player per team must be identified as a goalkeeper. Substitutions may be made in accordance with the rules of competition under which the game is being played. In youth games, substitution is commonly permitted, for either team, at the start of any period, after a goal is scored, and before a goal kick. Before a throw-in, only the team taking the throw may make a substitution.

Practical Considerations. A substitute may not enter the field of play until permitted by the referee.

A substitute may not enter the field of play until the player being replaced has left the field.

A substitution may be made only during certain stoppages of play in accordance with the rules of competition under which the game is being played.

Dividing the youth games into quarters provides additional stoppages of play in which coaches can make substitutions.

Modifications for Youth Play. Small-sided games are recommended for players below the age of 11 (Table 4-3).

Small-sided games provide more opportunities for involvement.

Small-sided games are not as complicated as full-sided games.

It is easier to coach a team with a smaller number of players.

Table 4-3. Recommended number of players per side and field dimensions.

Age (Years)	Players Per Side	Dimensions (in yards)	
		Width	Length
< 8	7	40–50	60–70*
8–10	7–9	50–60	70–80*
> 11	11	65–80	110–120

*Note that two small-sided cross field games could be played on a full-size (regulation) soccer field.

Law IV—Players' Equipment

Players on each team must wear similarly colored shirts to distinguish them from the opponents. A goalkeeper must wear a shirt of a different color from either team, opposing goalkeeper, and referee.

Shin guards are required. They must be covered entirely by the stockings. Coaches can instill the habit of wearing shin guards by insisting that players wear them during practices as well as games.

Court shoes or studded soccer shoes that conform to the rules of safety are permissible.

Molded Cleats

- The studs shall be made of rubber, plastic, polyurethene, or similar material.
- Each shoe shall have no fewer than 10 studs.
- The studs shall project no more than ¾ inch.
- The studs shall have a diameter of ⅜ inch or more.

Shoes with Replaceable Studs

- The studs shall be made of leather, rubber, aluminum, plastic, or similar material.
- The studs shall project no more than ¾ inch.
- The studs shall have a diameter of ½ inch or more.

Any player who does not meet the equipment requirements before the game is not permitted to play until these requirements are met.

Practical Considerations. Players must not wear anything that is dangerous to another player or to themselves.

Law V—Referees

One referee has full responsibility for the match. This person starts and stops play, keeps time, keeps score, and punishes teams for unfair play by giving the ball to the team that has been fouled. For serious infractions, the referee can disallow a player from continuing to play, resulting in the team playing one or more players short for the rest of the match. The referee's decisions are final. Common referee signals are illustrated in Figures 4-3 through 4-9.

Practical Considerations. The referee must be neutral and fair. The referee must be concerned for the safety of the players. Communication with the referee during play should be politely carried out by the team captain.

Modifications for Youth Play. In youth play, the referee should avoid stopping play by repeatedly calling trivial fouls. Judgment of intent must be made before a foul is whistled. Accidental or incidental contact is extremely

Figure 4-3. Penalty Kick—The referee points to the penalty kick mark to signal a penalty kick.

Figure 4-6. Corner Kick—The referee raises an arm and hand in the direction of the corner from which the kick is to be taken.

Figure 4-4. Goal Kick—The referee points to the half of the goal from which the goal kick is to be taken.

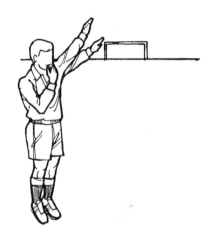

Figure 4-7. Substitution.

Figure 4-5. Play on/Advantage—This signifies that the referee has seen a foul, but chose not to call it because by doing so it would take away the advantage from the team fouled.

Figure 4-8. Indirect Free Kick—This signal should be held until the kick has been taken and the ball is played by another player or goes out of play.

Figure 4-9. Caution or Ejection—When the referee raises a yellow card a player or coach is being cautioned. If the card raised is red, that player or coach is being ejected from the game.

common; malicious behavior and the intent to injure rarely occur. Unimpeded play is important to the players' enjoyment of and commitment to the game.

On the other hand, referees must also be aware that injuries at the youth level are almost never feigned. When young players appear to be hurt or injured, the referee should stop the game immediately and allow qualified individuals to attend to them.

Whenever possible, the referee should explain the calls to the youth players. Referees of youth games must know the laws of the game in order to project this knowledge to young or inexperienced soccer players.

Law VI—Linespersons

Two linespersons assist the referee by indicating when the ball is out of play and which team puts it back into play by signaling for a throw-in, goal kick, corner kick, goal, or offside. However, final decisions are made by the referee. FIFA notes that it is the duty of the referee to act upon the information of neutral linespersons regarding incidents that were not personally noted by the referee. Linespersons assist with the match in any other way the referee deems important.

Common linespersons' signals are shown in Figures 4-10 through 4-17. The two linespersons and one referee compose a three-person officiating system. Communication among these three is critical to game control.

Practical Considerations. Linespersons must be neutral. Spectators must provide sufficient space along the sideline for the linespersons. Coaches and team officials should not allow spectators to interfere with any aspect of the game.

Figure 4-10. Throw-In—The team that attacks the goal in the direction that the flag is pointed receives the throw-in.

Figure 4-11. An offside has occurred.

Figure 4-12. Offside—After calling offside, the signal indicates that the offside occurred on the far side of the field.

Figure 4-15. Substitution.

Figure 4-13. After calling offside, this signal indicates that the offside occurred near the middle of the field.

Figure 4-16. Goal kick.

Figure 4-14. After calling offside, this signals that the offside occurred near the side of the field.

Figure 4-17. Corner kick.

Modifications for Youth Play. In some youth leagues, each team provides a linesperson (club linesperson). Under these circumstances, the linespersons signal only when the ball goes out of play. Some leagues use two referees who have equal responsibility for making decisions. Under this two-person officiating system, no linespersons are used.

- Club linespersons should be neutral.
- Club linespersons should not be allowed to flag for a foul or offside.

Law VII—Duration of the Game

A game is divided into equal halves. Adult matches last 90 minutes with a half-time interval of five minutes. Time shall be extended in either half for the taking of a penalty kick when the call was made before regulation time expired. Generally, ties will stand, since overtimes are only played in tournament or championship games.

Practical Considerations. The referee is the official timekeeper for the match.

The referee may extend play for time lost due to an injury, wasting of time by a team, or other conditions that interfere with either team playing a full match.

Modifications for Youth Play. The time period for a game should be modified for youth play (Table 4-4).

Dividing youth games into equal quarters permits coaches to make more substitutions and instruct players.

Table 4-4. Recommended duration of a game.

Age Group (Years)	Duration (Minutes)
< 8	40
8–10	50
11–12	60–70
13–14	70–80
> 14	80–90

Law VIII—The Start of Play

This law describes the methods and rules for starting play with a place kick and a drop ball.

Place Kick. Which team takes the place kick (kickoff) at the beginning of the game or over-

time is determined by a coin toss. The winner of the toss has a choice of either kicking off or selecting which goal to defend. Teams reverse sides to start the second half. A place kick is also used to restart play after a goal. It is taken by the team scored upon.

Drop Ball. If the referee must stop play for a reason not stated in the Laws of the Game, and the ball has not passed over one of the touch lines or goal lines immediately before play stopped, the game must be restarted by a drop ball where the ball was when play was stopped.

Practical Considerations. The referee does not need to wait for players from both teams to gather to drop the ball back into play. However, the ball should be dropped between two opposing players.

Players should be advised by the referee not to play the ball before it strikes the ground.

If the referee is uncertain which team last played the ball before it went over a touch line or goal line, play shall be restarted with a drop ball near where it went out of bounds.

Law IX—Ball In and Out of Play

The ball is out of play when it entirely crosses the goal line or touch line, or the referee stops the game. The ball is in play if it rebounds from a goal post, cross bar, or corner flag and stays within the field of play. It is in play if it rebounds from a referee or linesperson on the field and stays within the field of play.

Practical Consideration. Players should keep playing until the ball is completely over the goal line or touch line and the referee whistles to stop play.

Law X—Method of Scoring

The ball must go all the way over the goal line, under the cross bar, and between the goal posts for a goal to be scored (Figure 4-18).

Practical Consideration. Players should be coached to keep playing until the referee signals that a goal has been scored.

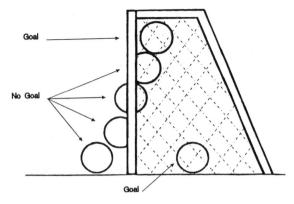

Figure 4-18. Goal or no goal.

Law XI—Offside

The offside rule is the most complex rule in soccer because of the contingencies and judgments associated with its application.

Offside Position

All of the following conditions must occur in order for a player to be in an offside position (Figure 4-19):

- offensive player in opponent's half of the field
- offensive player nearer to opponent's goal line than at least two opponents (An offensive player who is *even* with the second to last opponent or with the two last opponents is not in an offside position.)
- offensive player not in possession of the ball and closer to the opponent's goal line than the ball

Seeking to Gain an Advantage

In addition to being in an offside position, a player must be seeking to gain an advantage from the position by attempting to either play the ball or hinder or distract opposing players. However, if a player receives a ball directly from a throw-in, corner kick, goal kick, or drop ball, the player is not offside.

If a player is declared offside, an indirect free kick is taken by the opposing team from the position of the offside player.

Practical Consideration. Goals should be the result of skillful play rather than players standing in an offside position, in front of the opponent's goal, waiting to score.

Law XII—Fouls and Misconduct

Each of the four major sections of this law describes what is (or is not) permitted and the result of an infraction to a rule.

Legal Charge
The term "charge" describes allowed intentional contact between players. It:
- *must be shoulder to shoulder with arms (especially elbows) close to the body*
- *is permitted only while the ball is near enough to play*
- *must be intended to gain possession of the ball and not to knock down or injure an opponent, or be otherwise violent in nature*
- *is permitted when at least one foot of each player is in contact with the ground.*

Offensive Player	Offside Position?	Reasons(s)
O₁	Yes	Offensive player in opponent's half of the field
		Fewer than 2 defenders between offensive player and opponent's goal line
		Offensive player not in possession of the ball and closer to the opponent's goal line than the ball
O₂	No	Even with second to last defender (not closer to opponent's goal line than at least two defenders)
O₃	No	Offensive player is in possession of the ball
O₄	No	Offensive player in own half of the field

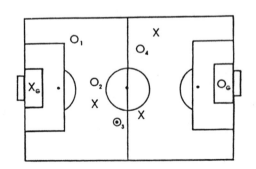

Figure 4-19. Offside position or not?

Section I—The Nine Penal Fouls. The nine penal fouls are the most serious fouls in soccer (Table 4-5). Four are committed by the arms, three are committed by the legs, and two are committed by the body.

Section II—The Five Non-Penal Fouls. The second section of Law XII deals with five less serious types of fouls described in Table 4-6.

Section III Cautionable Offenses. The third section of Law XII involves conduct or behavior that is considered unacceptable (Table 4-7). A referee designates a cautionable offense by holding up a yellow card to the player who committed the misconduct. A player who commits a second cautionable offense must be ejected.

Section IV—Ejectionable Offenses. The fourth section of Law XII involves more serious misconduct (Table 4-8). A referee designates an ejectionable offense by holding up a red card to the player who committed the act.

Practical Consideration. Soccer is a game that should be won through the use of skill. Law XII provides a framework for penalizing unacceptable actions that detract from the skill of playing the game.

Modifications for Youth Play. Penal and non-penal fouls, committed by young players, are often due to lack of knowledge about the rules of play or carelessness.

Referees must use careful judgment. Issuing either yellow or red cards must never be done in an accusatory or harsh fashion.

Law XIII—Free Kick

If a foul or misconduct occurs while the ball is in play, a free kick is awarded to the

Table 4-5. The nine penal fouls.

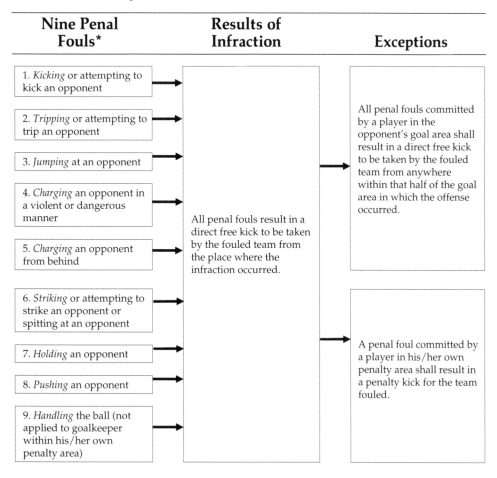

Nine Penal Fouls*	Results of Infraction	Exceptions
1. *Kicking* or attempting to kick an opponent		
2. *Tripping* or attempting to trip an opponent		All penal fouls committed by a player in the opponent's goal area shall result in a direct free kick to be taken by the fouled team from anywhere within that half of the goal area in which the offense occurred.
3. *Jumping* at an opponent		
4. *Charging* an opponent in a violent or dangerous manner	All penal fouls result in a direct free kick to be taken by the fouled team from the place where the infraction occurred.	
5. *Charging* an opponent from behind		
6. *Striking* or attempting to strike an opponent or spitting at an opponent		
7. *Holding* an opponent		A penal foul committed by a player in his/her own penalty area shall result in a penalty kick for the team fouled.
8. *Pushing* an opponent		
9. *Handling* the ball (not applied to goalkeeper within his/her own penalty area)		

* All penalty fouls, except handling, are fouls that are intentionally committed against an opponent.

Table 4-6. The five non-penal fouls.

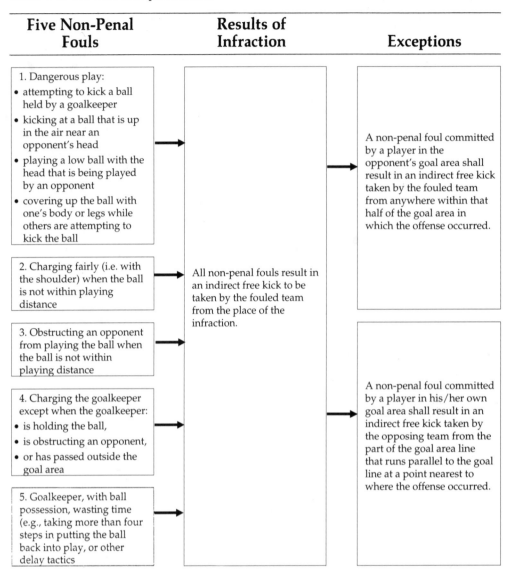

Five Non-Penal Fouls	Results of Infraction	Exceptions
1. Dangerous play: • attempting to kick a ball held by a goalkeeper • kicking at a ball that is up in the air near an opponent's head • playing a low ball with the head that is being played by an opponent • covering up the ball with one's body or legs while others are attempting to kick the ball	All non-penal fouls result in an indirect free kick to be taken by the fouled team from the place of the infraction.	A non-penal foul committed by a player in the opponent's goal area shall result in an indirect free kick taken by the fouled team from anywhere within that half of the goal area in which the offense occurred.
2. Charging fairly (i.e. with the shoulder) when the ball is not within playing distance		
3. Obstructing an opponent from playing the ball when the ball is not within playing distance		
4. Charging the goalkeeper except when the goalkeeper: • is holding the ball, • is obstructing an opponent, • or has passed outside the goal area		A non-penal foul committed by a player in his/her own goal area shall result in an indirect free kick taken by the opposing team from the part of the goal area line that runs parallel to the goal line at a point nearest to where the offense occurred.
5. Goalkeeper, with ball possession, wasting time (e.g., taking more than four steps in putting the ball back into play, or other delay tactics		

fouled team. Law XII (Fouls and Misconducts) refers to two types of free kicks—**Direct Free Kick** and **Indirect Free Kick** (Table 4-9). All free kicks are taken from where the foul occurred, unless the foul is committed in either team's goal area.

Direct Free Kick

A goal can be scored by kicking the ball directly into the opponent's goal without being touched or played by another player.

Indirect Free Kick

A goal can be scored only if the ball is touched or played by another player after it is kicked into play.

Practical Considerations. A player taking any free kick may choose to take the kick when opponents are closer than the rules permit to quickly return the ball to play.

A player taking any free kick may ask the referee to make defenders stay at least 10 yards from the point where the kick will be taken.

Table 4-7. Cautionable offenses.

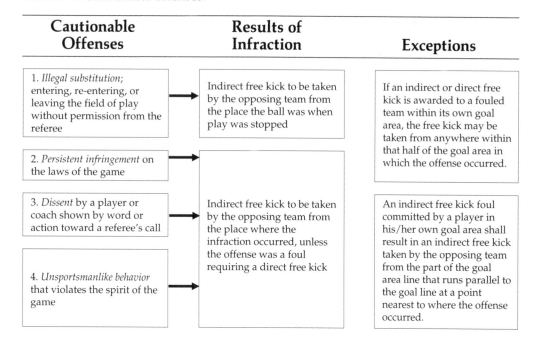

Cautionable Offenses	Results of Infraction	Exceptions
1. *Illegal substitution;* entering, re-entering, or leaving the field of play without permission from the referee	Indirect free kick to be taken by the opposing team from the place the ball was when play was stopped	If an indirect or direct free kick is awarded to a fouled team within its own goal area, the free kick may be taken from anywhere within that half of the goal area in which the offense occurred.
2. *Persistent infringement* on the laws of the game		
3. *Dissent* by a player or coach shown by word or action toward a referee's call	Indirect free kick to be taken by the opposing team from the place where the infraction occurred, unless the offense was a foul requiring a direct free kick	An indirect free kick foul committed by a player in his/her own goal area shall result in an indirect free kick taken by the opposing team from the part of the goal area line that runs parallel to the goal line at a point nearest to where the offense occurred.
4. *Unsportsmanlike behavior* that violates the spirit of the game		

Table 4-8. Ejectionable offenses.

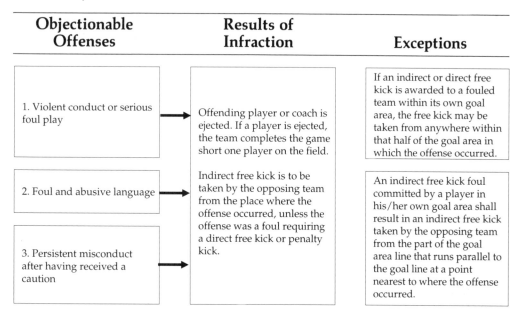

Objectionable Offenses	Results of Infraction	Exceptions
1. Violent conduct or serious foul play	Offending player or coach is ejected. If a player is ejected, the team completes the game short one player on the field.	If an indirect or direct free kick is awarded to a fouled team within its own goal area, the free kick may be taken from anywhere within that half of the goal area in which the offense occurred.
2. Foul and abusive language	Indirect free kick is to be taken by the opposing team from the place where the offense occurred, unless the offense was a foul requiring a direct free kick or penalty kick.	An indirect free kick foul committed by a player in his/her own goal area shall result in an indirect free kick taken by the opposing team from the part of the goal area line that runs parallel to the goal line at a point nearest to where the offense occurred.
3. Persistent misconduct after having received a caution		

Encroachment on free kicks (i.e., not backing up 10 yards right away) is a cautionable offense and may result in a yellow card being issued.

The spirit of fair play dictates that opponents not interfere with the other team's ability to put the ball into play from a free kick.

Table 4-9. Conditional applications of free kick rules.

Conditions	Requirements	Results of Infraction
Any free kick	The ball must be stationary before being kicked into play.	The free kick is retaken.
	When the ball is put into play, it cannot be touched or played a second time by the player taking the free kick until another player has touched or played the ball.	An indirect free kick, to be taken from the location of the infraction, is awarded to the opposing team.
	A player cannot put the ball into play and score directly on his/her own goal.	The goal does not count and a corner kick is awarded to the opposing team.
Any free kick taken from inside own penalty area	The ball is in play when it has moved a distance equal to its circumference and is inside the field beyond the penalty area.	The free kick is retaken.
	The goalkeeper may not receive the free kick directly into his/her hands in the penalty area.	
	* Opposing players must be 10 yards from the ball at the time of the kick and must remain outside the penalty area until the ball has passed out of the penalty area.	Opposing players may be cautioned for unsporting conduct. If cautioned, the free kick is retaken.
Any free kick taken from outside own goal area	The ball is in play when it has moved a distance equal to its circumference.	The free kick is retaken.
	*Opposing players must be 10 yards from the ball until it is played, unless they are standing on their own goal line between the goal posts.	Opposing players may be cautioned for unsporting conduct. If cautioned, the free kick is retaken.
Any free kick taken from inside own goal area	The free kick may be taken from anywhere within that half of the goal area in which the offense occurred.	The free kick is retaken from within the appropriate half of the goal area.
Any indirect free kick taken inside own goal area	The indirect free kick cannot be used to score directly on an opponent's goal.	A goal kick is awarded to the opposing team.
	The indirect free kick cannot be used to score directly on player's own goal.	A corner kick is awarded to the opposing team.
Any indirect free kick awarded taken within opponents' goal area	The indirect free kick must be taken from the part of the goal area line that runs parallel to the goal line at a point nearest to where the offense occurred.	The indirect free kick is retaken.

*See following Practical Considerations.

Law XIV—Penalty Kick

A penalty kick is awarded to the offended team when one of the nine penal fouls (see Law XII—Fouls and Misconduct) is intentionally committed by a player in his/her own penalty area. It should be noted that the location of the penal foul, not the location of the ball, determines whether a penalty kick is awarded. For a penalty kick, the ball is placed on the penalty mark and a goal can be scored directly from the kick. If a penalty kick is awarded just before half-time or full-time, that period is extended for the taking of the penalty kick. For any penalty kick, if the kicked ball is deflected into the goal from the goal posts, cross bar, or goalkeeper, the goal is counted. However, during an extension of time for the taking of a penalty kick, no time is permitted for the kicker or any other person to follow up on a rebounding ball. See Table 4-10 for details.

Practical Considerations. Because a penalty kick is an excellent scoring opportunity, overt distractions by either the kicker or goalkeeper must not be allowed.

Spectators and coaches should remain in designated areas (e.g., outside the field and between the two penalty areas) throughout the game. They should not be allowed behind the goal, especially when a penalty kick is being taken.

Law XV—Throw-In

A throw-in is awarded when the entire ball passes over the touch line (ball in touch) on the ground or in the air (see Law IX, Ball In and Out of Play). The throw-in is awarded to the team that did not touch the ball last. The ball is back in play when it enters the field from a proper throw-in (Table 4-11).

Practical Consideration. The purpose of the throw-in is to quickly restart play. It should not be used to delay the game or to gain an unfair advantage.

Law XVI—Goal Kick

A non-soring ball, which was played or touched last by a player on the attacking team over his/her opponent's goal line, is put back into play by the defending team taking a goal kick (Table 4-12). The entire ball must pass beyond the goal line, either on the ground or in the air, in order for a goal kick to be awarded (see Law IX—Ball In and Out of Play). The ball is put back into play from a point anywhere within that half of the goal area nearest to where it went out of play.

Practical Considerations. The player taking a goal kick may choose to take the kick when opponents are inside the penalty area to quickly return the ball to play.

The player taking a goal kick may ask the referee to ensure proper positioning of opponents.

Law XVII—Corner Kick

A non-scoring ball, which was played or touched last by a player on the defending team over his/her own goal line, is returned to play from a corner kick by the attacking team. The entire ball must pass beyond the goal line, either on the ground or in the air, in order for a corner kick to be awarded (see Law IX—Ball In and Out of Play). *The whole of the ball must be placed entirely within the quarter-circle nearest the point where the ball went out of play. The corner flag must not be displaced in order to facilitate the taking of a corner kick. A goal may be scored directly from a corner kick (Table 4-13).*

Practical Considerations. The player taking a corner kick may choose to take the kick when opponents are closer than the rules permit to quickly return the ball to play.

The player taking the corner kick may ask the referee to ensure proper positioning of opponents.

Table 4-10. Conditional applications of penalty kick rules.

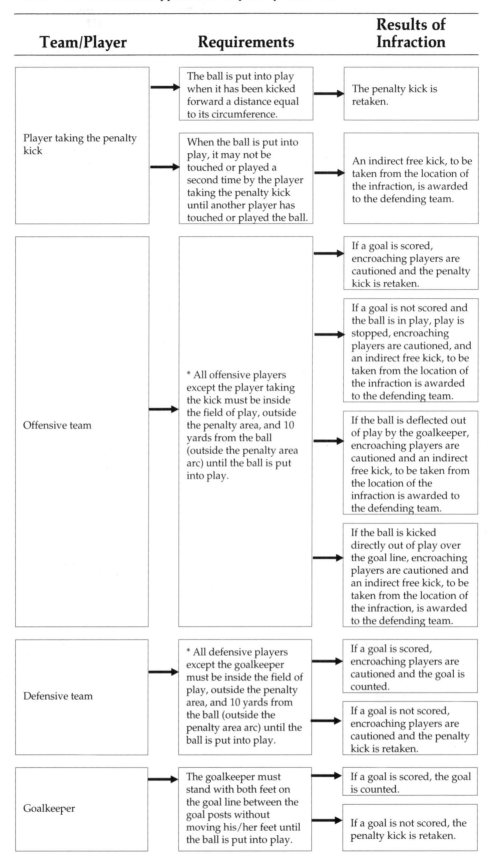

Team/Player	Requirements	Results of Infraction
Player taking the penalty kick	The ball is put into play when it has been kicked forward a distance equal to its circumference.	The penalty kick is retaken.
	When the ball is put into play, it may not be touched or played a second time by the player taking the penalty kick until another player has touched or played the ball.	An indirect free kick, to be taken from the location of the infraction, is awarded to the defending team.
Offensive team	* All offensive players except the player taking the kick must be inside the field of play, outside the penalty area, and 10 yards from the ball (outside the penalty area arc) until the ball is put into play.	If a goal is scored, encroaching players are cautioned and the penalty kick is retaken.
		If a goal is not scored and the ball is in play, play is stopped, encroaching players are cautioned, and an indirect free kick, to be taken from the location of the infraction is awarded to the defending team.
		If the ball is deflected out of play by the goalkeeper, encroaching players are cautioned and an indirect free kick, to be taken from the location of the infraction is awarded to the defending team.
		If the ball is kicked directly out of play over the goal line, encroaching players are cautioned and an indirect free kick, to be taken from the location of the infraction, is awarded to the defending team.
Defensive team	* All defensive players except the goalkeeper must be inside the field of play, outside the penalty area, and 10 yards from the ball (outside the penalty area arc) until the ball is put into play.	If a goal is scored, encroaching players are cautioned and the goal is counted.
		If a goal is not scored, encroaching players are cautioned and the penalty kick is retaken.
Goalkeeper	The goalkeeper must stand with both feet on the goal line between the goal posts without moving his/her feet until the ball is put into play.	If a goal is scored, the goal is counted.
		If a goal is not scored, the penalty kick is retaken.

* NOTE: If both offensive and defensive players encroach on the taking of a penalty kick, encroaching players are cautioned and the penalty kick is retaken irrespective of the outcome of the kick.

Table 4-11. Conditional applications of throw-in rules.

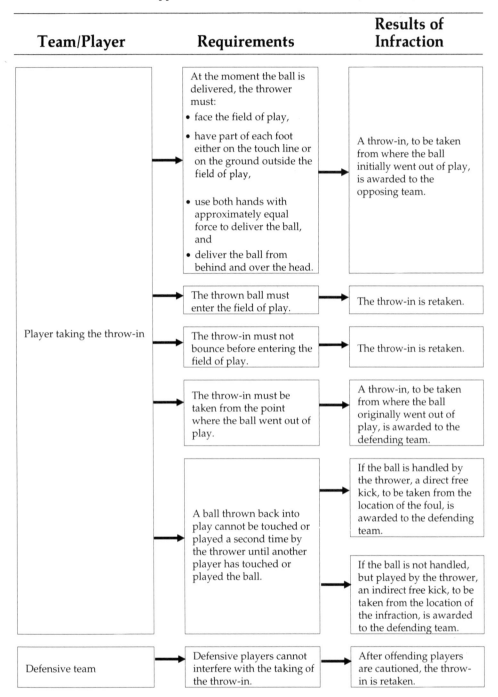

Team/Player	Requirements	Results of Infraction
Player taking the throw-in	At the moment the ball is delivered, the thrower must: • face the field of play, • have part of each foot either on the touch line or on the ground outside the field of play, • use both hands with approximately equal force to deliver the ball, and • deliver the ball from behind and over the head.	A throw-in, to be taken from where the ball initially went out of play, is awarded to the opposing team.
	The thrown ball must enter the field of play.	The throw-in is retaken.
	The throw-in must not bounce before entering the field of play.	The throw-in is retaken.
	The throw-in must be taken from the point where the ball went out of play.	A throw-in, to be taken from where the ball originally went out of play, is awarded to the defending team.
	A ball thrown back into play cannot be touched or played a second time by the thrower until another player has touched or played the ball.	If the ball is handled by the thrower, a direct free kick, to be taken from the location of the foul, is awarded to the defending team. If the ball is not handled, but played by the thrower, an indirect free kick, to be taken from the location of the infraction, is awarded to the defending team.
Defensive team	Defensive players cannot interfere with the taking of the throw-in.	After offending players are cautioned, the throw-in is retaken.

Table 4-12. Conditional applications of goal kick rules.

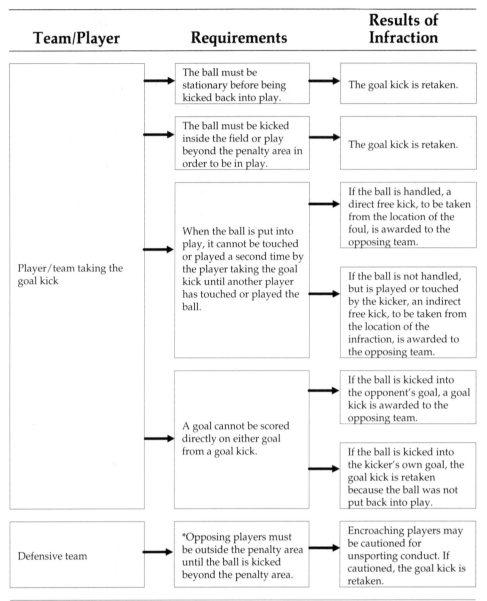

Team/Player	Requirements	Results of Infraction
Player/team taking the goal kick	The ball must be stationary before being kicked back into play.	The goal kick is retaken.
	The ball must be kicked inside the field or play beyond the penalty area in order to be in play.	The goal kick is retaken.
	When the ball is put into play, it cannot be touched or played a second time by the player taking the goal kick until another player has touched or played the ball.	If the ball is handled, a direct free kick, to be taken from the location of the foul, is awarded to the opposing team.
		If the ball is not handled, but is played or touched by the kicker, an indirect free kick, to be taken from the location of the infraction, is awarded to the opposing team.
	A goal cannot be scored directly on either goal from a goal kick.	If the ball is kicked into the opponent's goal, a goal kick is awarded to the opposing team.
		If the ball is kicked into the kicker's own goal, the goal kick is retaken because the ball was not put back into play.
Defensive team	*Opposing players must be outside the penalty area until the ball is kicked beyond the penalty area.	Encroaching players may be cautioned for unsporting conduct. If cautioned, the goal kick is retaken.

* See Practical Considerations.

Table 4-13. Conditional applications of corner kick rules.

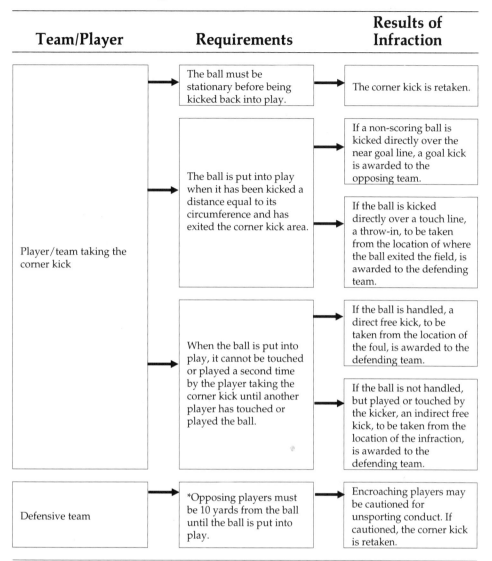

Team/Player	Requirements	Results of Infraction
Player/team taking the corner kick	The ball must be stationary before being kicked back into play.	The corner kick is retaken.
	The ball is put into play when it has been kicked a distance equal to its circumference and has exited the corner kick area.	If a non-scoring ball is kicked directly over the near goal line, a goal kick is awarded to the opposing team.
		If the ball is kicked directly over a touch line, a throw-in, to be taken from the location of where the ball exited the field, is awarded to the defending team.
	When the ball is put into play, it cannot be touched or played a second time by the player taking the corner kick until another player has touched or played the ball.	If the ball is handled, a direct free kick, to be taken from the location of the foul, is awarded to the defending team.
		If the ball is not handled, but played or touched by the kicker, an indirect free kick, to be taken from the location of the infraction, is awarded to the defending team.
Defensive team	*Opposing players must be 10 yards from the ball until the ball is put into play.	Encroaching players may be cautioned for unsporting conduct. If cautioned, the corner kick is retaken.

* See Practical Considerations.

5
Kicking

INTRODUCTION

In the sport of soccer, kicking is used to pass or shoot the ball. Distance, speed, and accuracy are the three key elements of kicking. Their importance varies with the conditions of play.

There are several individual techniques for kicking the soccer ball. However, the four kicking components—approach, pre-impact, impact, and follow-through—are all relevant to any kicking technique.

This chapter and the other soccer skills chapters provide background information for parents and volunteer coaches, but young players need lots of trial-and-error opportunities to discover how kicking works—and how to become better kickers. Simple practices that promote kicking repetitions through passing, shooting, and dribbling in small-sided scrimmages will ensure that players are having fun and learning the basics through self-discovery. Let the game teach the kids!

These details and diagrams give coaches and parents material for the occasional BRIEF teaching point or demonstration. Emulating and copying your movements are natural methods through which your players will acquire soccer skills.

FOUR COMPONENTS OF KICKING

Approach

A player's movement toward the ball before kicking is the approach. The manner in which this is performed affects the outcome of the kick. A full-speed run to the ball is rarely desirable, because a player will not likely be able to control the kick. There are two types of approaches: straight and angled.

Straight Approach. In a straight approach, the player's path to the ball is in alignment with the direction of the intended path of the kicked ball (Figure 5-1). One exception to this is the outside of the foot kick.

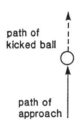

path of kicked ball

path of approach

STRAIGHT APPROACH

Figure 5-1. Path of the straight approach.

Angled Approach. In an angled approach, the player's path to the ball is not in alignment with the direction of the intended path of the kicked ball. An angled approach may range from a straight line to a curved path (Figure 5-2).

The last step of an approach, whether straight or angled, should be a leap. A leap provides time for and aids in the backswing of the kicking leg (Figure 5-3). During a leap, the knee of the kicking leg should be flexing and the hip of the kicking leg should be extending. The de-

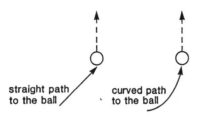

straight path
to the ball
curved path
to the ball

ANGLED APPROACH
(right–foot kick)

Figure 5-2. Path of the angled approach.

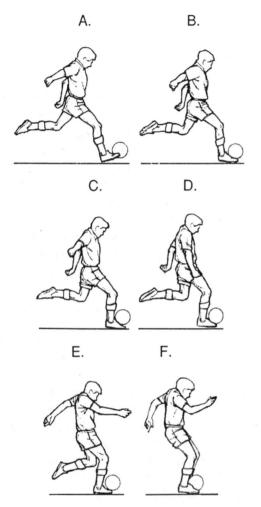

A.   B.

C.   D.

E.   F.

Figure 5-3. Side view of approach.

gree of flexing and extending should be related to the desired ball velocity. For maximum ball velocity, the hip should be fully extended before the player swings the kicking leg forward.

Pre-Impact

Pre-impact follows an approach. It begins with the placement of the supporting foot on the ground, at the end of the leap (Figure 5-4), and ends immediately before the kicking foot impacts the ball. As a player contacts the ground, the support leg acts like a strut: to block the forward movement of its hip, to start the forward rotation of the other hip, and to initiate forward swing of the thigh of the kicking leg. The knee of the kicking leg continues to flex. Just before impact, the speed of the

Figure 5-4. Pre-Impact.

thigh's forward rotation should rapidly decrease as the knee of the kicking leg quickly extends.

The arms counterbalance the forceful forward swing of the kicking leg. The arms are generally held out to the sides of the body. As the kicking leg swings forward, the arm on the same side of the body swings back and the arm on the opposite side swings forward. The function of the arms to counter-balance the action of the kicking leg continues through impact and follow through.

Two factors in an angled approach enhance its potential to maximize ball velocity: *an open hip position* and the *use of a longer lever.*

Hip Position. The hip of the kicking leg is drawn farther back, or is more open, at the start of the pre-impact in an angled approach than it is in a straight approach (Figure 5-5). As a consequence, the kicking leg can move forward with greater velocity.

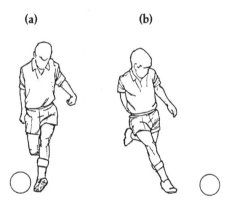

Figure 5-5. Position of the hip of the kicking leg at the start of pre-impact: (a) closed hip position in straight approach, (b) opened hip position in angled approach.

Lever Length. In an angled approach, the support foot is farther from the side of the ball than it is in a straight approach (Figure 5-6). The trunk leans away from the ball, allowing the player to fully extend the kicking leg (lever) when impacting the ball. In the straight approach, the knee of the kicking leg must be bent so the foot can clear the ground. The longer lever in the angled approach provides for potentially greater ball velocity.

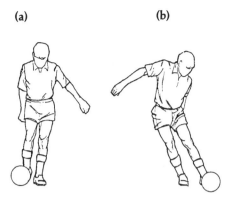

Figure 5-6. Lever length at impact in a straight (a) and an angled approach (b).

Impact

Five factors influence how the ball is projected from the foot: placement of the support foot, trunk lean, point of impact, firmness of impact, and area of foot contact.

Placement of the Support Foot. If the support foot is to the side and front of the ball, the kicking foot will likely make contact with the ball on the downswing and compress the ball against the ground. If the support foot is alongside the ball, contact will be made at the bottom of the arc of the kicking foot, resulting in a low drive. Support foot placement to the side and behind the ball will cause the ball to be struck on the upswing of the kicking foot, lifting the ball into the air.

Trunk Lean. The lean of the trunk is usually associated with support foot placement. The farther behind the ball the support foot is placed, the farther back the trunk tends to lean to help the kicking foot reach the ball. As the support foot is positioned farther forward, the trunk tends to be more upright.

Point of Impact. Figure 5-7 represents the effect of the point of impact on the subsequent projection of the ball.

The spin and resulting curve imparted to the ball can be increased by an oblique or off-center kick of the ball. This is known as "bending the ball" or "swerving the ball." It is useful in projecting a ball around a defender who has "closed space" and in kicking a ball around a defensive wall when taking a free kick.

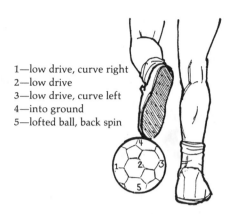

1—low drive, curve right
2—low drive
3—low drive, curve left
4—into ground
5—lofted ball, back spin

Figure 5-7. Location of impact and resulting projection of the ball.

Firmness of Impact. If the ankle and foot of the kicking leg are held firm on impact, the ball will attain a greater velocity than if the foot is loosely held.

Area of Foot Contact. As the area of foot contact with the ball increases, ball control increases accordingly. Thus, players can better control the direction of an instep kick than they can the direction of a toe kick.

Follow-Through

The movement of the body immediately after the completion of impact is the follow-through, when the speed of the kicking leg is decreased and controlled. During this time the player should gain control of body movements to proceed to subsequent activity.

The follow-through is the result of the approach, pre-impact, and impact, so the coach will need to observe and analyze how the body parts move during the follow-through.

INDIVIDUAL TECHNIQUES

There are many ways to kick a soccer ball. Variations depend upon the part of the foot that impacts the ball, the location of the foot's impact on the ball, the direction of movement of the foot during impact, and the location of the ball (ground, half volley, or air). The remainder of this chapter will present various techniques of kicking based on parts of the foot hitting the ball.

Inside of the Foot Kicks

The inside of the foot is used to kick the ball relatively short distances (Figures 5-8 to 5-10). It is the most accurate type of kick because a large surface area of the foot contacts the ball. This kick can be used to accurately shoot the ball on goal from short distances and to make short, controlled passes to teammates.

Figure 5-8. Inside of the foot kick on a ground ball (push pass).

Figure 5-9. Driving a ball low from a half volley with the inside of the foot kick.

Figure 5-10. Swerving a ball from a half volley with the inside of the instep and inside of the foot kick.

Instep Kicks

The instep kick is the most powerful kick in soccer. It is used to kick the ball long distances or with considerable pace. This kick can be used to make powerful kicks on goal from short or long distances and to make long passes to teammates.

Beginners often have difficulty learning the instep kick for several reasons.

- It requires coordination of rapidly moving body parts.
- It requires accurate foot placement and body positioning.
- They perceive previously learned "toe" kicking as initially more successful and are, therefore, reluctant to use the instep kick.
- They are anxious about the possibility of an injury from kicking the ground.

The following five-step approach can be used to help beginning soccer players refine the instep kick. However, trial-and-error and self-discovery should be encouraged **first!**

Step 1—Manual Guidance. A key factor in the success of any kick in soccer is the placement of the supporting foot (the non-kicking, planted foot). Manual guidance of the kicking leg (Figure 5-11) minimizes this problem because the ball is placed by the coach directly to the side of the support foot after the support foot has been positioned. The player maintains balance on the support foot by holding the shoulders of the coach. This supported position properly aligns the head and trunk of the player over the ball. The athlete must flex the hip of the kicking leg just enough for the extended foot to clear the ground during the leg swing. The coach holds the ball with one hand from

behind and guides the player's kicking leg back and forth, flexing and extending the athlete's knee. The extended instep should contour to the ball and be guided in making firm contact.

Figure 5-11. Coach and player positioning during manual guidance.

Step 2—Supported Kick. The next phase is the supported kick (Figure 5-12). This can be attempted after only a few minutes of practice with manual guidance. It differs from the manual guidance technique in that the player controls the kicking motion of the leg and foot contact. Support is still maintained by placing the hands on the shoulders of the coach. The coach positions the ball directly to the side of the support foot. The player must control the force of the kick. The intent of this phase is not to teach forceful kicking, but to teach leg control, proper foot contact (contour with the ball), and proper body alignment.

Step 3—Leap Kick. Once the player demonstrates control of the kicking leg in the supported kicking phase, the athlete should add a step onto the support foot before kicking. This step should become exaggerated into a short leap (Figure 5-13). Again, the force of the kick

Figure 5-12. Coach and player positioning during supported kicking.

must be controlled by the athlete. The coach holds the ball with both hands. The coach should provide feedback about the leap, support foot positioning, leg swing, body positioning, and instep contact with the ball.

Figure 5-13. Coach and player positioning during leap kick.

Step 4—Straight Approach. As control of the leap and kicking action progresses, the player should precede the leap by a few approach steps from directly behind the ball (Figure 5-14).

Figure 5-14. Placement of the support foot and path of the kicking foot in a low drive with the instep kick from a straight approach.

Step 5—Angled Approach. The final phase in this progression is to refine the angled approach to the ball. When the player kicks with the right foot, the approach should be from behind and to the left of the ball; when the player kicks with the left foot, the approach is made from behind and to the right of the ball. The straight and angled approach differ in two ways. First, the support foot is planted farther from the ball in the angled position (Figure 5-15), but it is still positioned directly to the side of it. Second, the hip and knee of the kicking leg do not need to be flexed for the extended foot to clear the ground. The body leans away from the ball, allowing the kicking leg to fully extend into impact.

Figure 5-15. Instep kick following an angled approach.

Figures 5-16 to 5-21 illustrate further applications of the instep kick.

Figure 5-16. Foot position when chipping the ball with the instep.

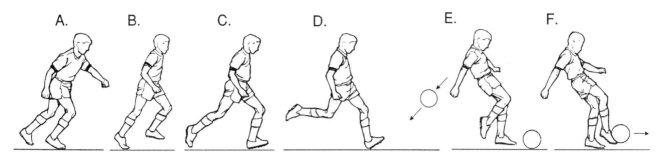

Figure 5-17. Use of the instep kick to drive the ball low from a half volley.

Figure 5-18. Proper kicking foot position during follow-through in the instep kick. The ankle is fully extended.

Figure 5-19. Side volley with the instep.

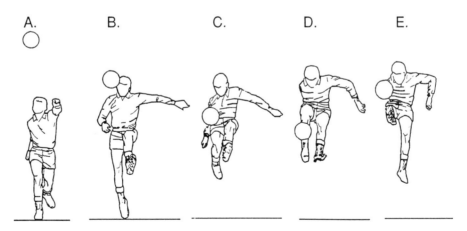

Figure 5-20. Front scissors kick with the instep.

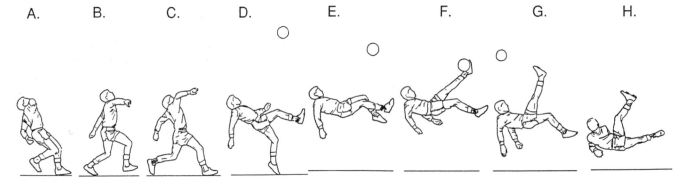

Figure 5-21. Overhead scissors kick.

Outside of the Foot Kicks

It is relatively difficult to control a kick with the outside of the foot because ball contact involves a glancing strike with the small area on the outside of the foot (Figure 5-22). This type of impact imparts spin to the ball and projects it laterally to the line of the leg swing (Figure 5-23). The direction of leg swing and ball projection are not the same, so the outside of the foot kick can be used to deceive opponents.

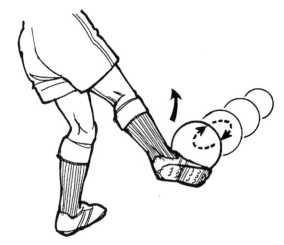

Figure 5-23. Ball spin and projection resulting from an outside of the foot kick with the right foot.

Figures 5-24 and 5-25 illustrate additional points about the outside of the foot kick.

Figure 5-22. Outside of the foot kick.

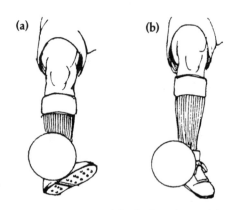

Figure 5-24. Orientation of the kicking leg and foot when lofting or swerving a ball with the outside of the foot on a half volley. (a) Lofted kick, (b) Swerved kick.

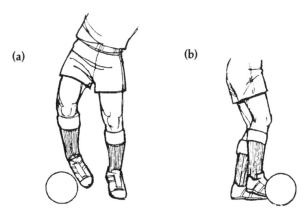

Figure 5-25. (a) Proper body orientation and leg swing for the outside of the foot kick. (b) Improper body orientation and leg swing.

Heel Pass (Back-Heel)

In this pass, the player uses the heel to kick a ground ball backward to a trailing teammate. The player can deceive an opponent into thinking the ball will be kicked forward. To perform the kick the player steps over the ball with the kicking foot, then flexes the knee in order to strike the ball with the heel (Figure 5-26).

Toe Kick (Toe Poke)

Many beginning players use the toes of their shoes to kick because they have not learned other individual kicking techniques. Although the uses of the toe kick in soccer are limited, it is helpful whenever there is not enough time for a full backswing. For example, when a ground ball is away from a player and closer to an opponent, the player can extend the leg and ankle to poke the ball away. It is also an excellent kick for scoring at close range.

PROGRESSION FOR TEACHING KICKING

As they play, practice, and refine their kicking skills, soccer players will progress from the easier to the more difficult skills. Table 5-1 includes a list of kicking techniques, rated by level of difficulty. Coaches and parents can use it as a general guide to determine a rough sequence in which kicking skills should be taught. Remember: Let the game teach the kids!

A.   B.   C.   D.   E.   F.

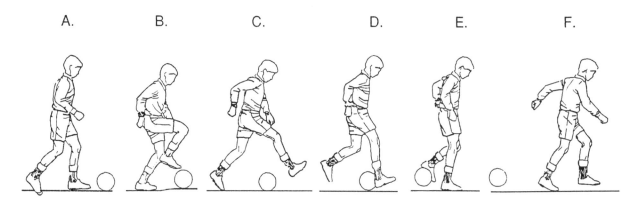

Figure 5-26. Back-heel on a rolling ball.

Table 5-1. Kicking—Difficulty Rating Form.

Level of Player* Approximate Age*	Suggested Emphasis		
	Beginning 6–9 yrs.	Intermediate 10–13 yrs.	Advanced 14 yrs. & up
Individual Techniques			
Inside of the foot kicks			
ground ball			
low drive	X	X	X
half volley			
low drive		X	X
lofted ball		X	X
swerved ball		X	X
air ball			
low drive	X	X	X
lofted ball	X	X	X
"chip"		X	X
swerved ball		X	X
half volley			
low drive		X	X
lofted ball		X	X
swerved ball			X
air ball			
low drive	X	X	X
lofted ball	X	X	X
swerved ball			X
side volley			X
front scissors			X
overhead scissors			X
over-the-shoulder scissors			X
Outside of the foot kicks			
ground ball			
low drive	X	X	X
half volley			
low drive			X
lofted ball			X
swerved ball			X
air ball			
low drive			X
lofted ball			X
swerved ball			X
Heel pass (back-heel)		X	X
Toe kick		X	X

*Note that "Beginning," "Intermediate," and "Advanced" does not always correspond with the age range given beneath it. Coaches should use this classification system as an approximation, adjusting the techniques to suit their players' ability levels. Experimentation is encouraged but *mastery* of the "basics" is the focus for technical training.

6
Receiving and Controlling

INTRODUCTION

In soccer, the ball is received as a result of an intended pass, an errant pass, a deflection, or an interception. The purpose of receiving the ball is to gain control of it in order to pass, dribble, or shoot.

There are many different ways to receive a soccer ball. Regardless of how the ball is received, four fundamental principles are involved: positioning, selecting, decreasing speed, and redirecting. Young players need lots of trial-and-error opportunities to discover how to receive and control. Simple practices that promote receiving repetitions through passing, shooting, and dribbling in small-sided scrimmages will ensure that players are having fun and learning the basics through self-discovery. Let the game teach the kids!

The details and diagrams in this chapter give coaches and parents material for the occasional BRIEF teaching point or demonstration. Emulating and copying your movements are natural methods through which players will acquire soccer skills.

FOUR FUNDAMENTALS OF RECEIVING

Positioning

Players should learn to move quickly to position to receive the ball to gain more time in which to make situational adjustments. Moving to position, when opponents are near, usually requires movement toward the ball.

Selecting

Different techniques can be used to receive a soccer ball. While moving to position, a player must select a technique according to several factors:

- path of the ball (steep to shallow arc)
- direction of the ball (toward or away from the body or across the midline of the body)
- level of the ball (rolling, half volley, or air ball)
- position and movement of opponents
- intended activity after receiving the ball
- ability of the player

Decreasing Speed

When receiving, it is usually desirable to decrease the speed of the ball for better control. Cushioning and wedging are the two methods of decreasing the speed of a ball.

Cushioning. Cushioning occurs when a relaxed body part absorbs and yields to the impact of the ball. Several different body parts may cushion the ball.

Wedging. Wedging usually involves lodging the ball between the surface of the foot and the ground to absorb the ball's impact.

Redirecting

The goal of redirecting is to move the ball into open space to gain additional time in which to control, pass, dribble, shoot, or move the ball into positions that will threaten the defense. The ball's direction after contact with a body part depends upon several factors at the moment of contact:

- point of contact with the ball
- orientation and direction of movement of the body part
- direction of movement of the ball
- positioning of nearby defenders

INDIVIDUAL TECHNIQUES

Receiving a Rolling Ball

All techniques for receiving a rolling ball involve the feet. A rolling ball is relatively easy to receive and control because it may be played anywhere along its path. A player usually has ample time to judge the movement of the ball and to get into position.

Players should learn to lift the receiving foot as the ball arrives. If the receiving foot is lifted too early, balance must be maintained on the support foot. From this position, adjustments to ball movements and opponents cannot be made. This is a common error in youth players just learning to receive rolling balls, half volleys, and some air balls. As a ball is received, the foot and ankle should be relaxed and moving in the same direction as the ball (Figure 6-1). If the foot strikes into the ball, the ball tends to rebound from the foot, making control more difficult.

Figure 6-1. Receiving a rolling ball with the inside of the foot. Note that the ball and the receiving foot are moving in the same direction.

Figures 6-2 and 6-3 illustrate additional techniques for receiving the ball.

The following sequential approach can be used to teach the various techniques to receive, control, and redirect rolling balls. The sequence is based on the players' progression from mastery of the fundamentals, to refinement in game-related activities, to performance under game conditions. As players get comfortable at each level, coaches adjust the amount of time, space, and pressure on the players.

Fundamentals
↓
Game-related Activities
↓
Game Conditions

1. Perform the proper movement pattern of a designated technique on a ball that is not moving.
2. Move to position and use a designated technique to receive and control a slowly passed ball.
3. Move to position and use a designated technique to receive and control a ball passed with considerable speed.
4. Move to position and use a designated technique to receive, control, and redirect a ball passed with considerable speed.
5. Move to position and select and perform an appropriate receiving, controlling, and redirecting technique on balls passed in various directions.
6. Move to position and select and perform an appropriate receiving, controlling, and redirecting technique when pressured by a defender.

Receiving a Half Volley

A ball that is in the air and then played immediately after striking the ground is referred to as a half volley. All techniques for receiving a half volley involve the feet. As a group, techniques for receiving half volleys are moderately difficult because the ball is usually moving relatively fast. Reception is limited to the short period of time immediately after the ball strikes the ground.

Errors that often occur in any of the techniques used to receive a half volley include the following:

- lifting the receiving foot too early
- striking at the ball
- failing to control the ball—When receiving, it is often important to play a ball the first time

Figure 6-2. Receiving a rolling ball with the inside of the foot and redirecting it between the legs ("out the back door")

Figure 6-3. Receiving a rolling ball with the outside of the foot.

it strikes the ground. If a ball bounces additional times before it is received with a half volley technique, it may be intercepted by an opponent.

• improper positioning—Beginning players will have difficulty judging where to position themselves in order to receive half volleys. A beginning player tends to move to a position too far from where the ball will strike the ground. From this position, the player will either overextend the leg to reach the ball or allow the ball to bounce too high before receiving it. When practicing half volley techniques with youth players, project the ball high enough to allow a receiving player to judge where the ball will strike the ground and to move to position.

The following sequential approach can be used to teach the various techniques used to receive, control, and redirect half volleys. Remember: Move from fundamentals to game-related activities to game conditions.

1. Use designated half volley techniques to receive and control balls that are tossed short distances.

2. Use designated half volley techniques to receive, control, and redirect balls that are tossed short distances.

3. Move to position and use designated half volley techniques to receive, control, and redirect balls that are tossed short distances.

4. Move to position and use designated half volley techniques to receive, control, and redirect balls that are tossed or kicked long distances.

5. Move to position and select and perform appropriate receiving, controlling, and redirecting techniques on balls that are passed or kicked in various directions.

6. Move to position and select and perform appropriate receiving, controlling, and redirecting techniques when pressured by a defender.

Receiving a Ball in the Air

A ball in the air is difficult to receive because it is usually moving relatively fast, there is only a short time in which to intercept its path, and additional reception techniques must be used when it rebounds to the ground. Figures 6-4 to 6-14 illustrate various techniques for receiving a ball in the air, including several that involve use of the thigh, chest, and head. (Caution: See Chapter 8 for limitations on the use of the head in soccer for young children.)

By substituting air balls for half volleys, the progression for coaching players to receive, control, and redirect a half volley can be followed in teaching the air ball techniques.

Figure 6-4. Receiving a ball in the air with the inside of the foot.

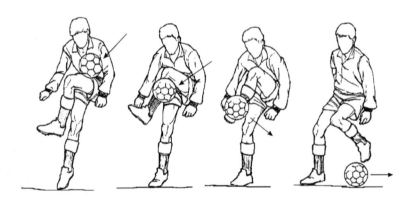

Figure 6-5. Receiving a ball in the air with the outside of the foot.

Figure 6-6. Receiving a ball in the air with the instep.

Figure 6-7. Receiving a ball in the air with the inside of the thigh.

Figure 6-8. Receiving a ball in the air with the top of the thigh.

Figure 6-9. Receiving a ball with a low trajectory with the top of the thigh.

Figure 6-10. Receiving a ball in the air with the chest.

Figure 6-11. Arm position permitted for girls when receiving the ball with the chest.

Figure 6-12. Receiving a ball in the air with the chest and redirecting it backward ("touch and turn").

Figure 6-13. Receiving a ball with the chest and redirecting it backward ("over the top").

Figure 6-14. Receiving a ball in the air with the head.

PROGRESSIONS FOR TEACHING RECEPTION AND CONTROL

Balls must be passed by throwing or kicking to players who are learning to receive and control. Coaches decide whether to throw or kick based on two factors: 1) where the balls need to go and 2) the skill levels of the players.

Table 6-1 includes a list of receiving and controlling techniques, rated by level of difficulty. Coaches and parents can use it as a general guide to determine a rough sequence in which these skills should be taught. Remember: let the game teach the kids!

Rolling Balls

Beginners should learn all the techniques for receiving and controlling rolling balls. Many players are able to make accurate passes to partners with the inside foot or the instep kicks. Initially with 6- and 7-year-old players, coaches may need to make passes themselves or have players roll balls with their hands. As kicking skills improve, players can begin passing and receiving with their feet.

Half Volleys and Air Balls

It is difficult for most new youth players to kick balls accurately to partners practicing half volley or air ball receptions; therefore, balls should be thrown. As skills are mastered, practices should include more half volley and air ball receptions with kicked balls.

Table 6-1. Receiving and Controlling—Difficulty Rating Form.

Level of Player* Approximate Age*	Suggested Emphasis		
	Beginning 6–9 yrs.	**Intermediate 10–13 yrs.**	**Advanced 14 yrs. & up**
Individual Techniques			
Rolling Ball			
sole of the foot	X	X	
inside of the foot	X	X	
redirecting forward	X	X	
"touch and turn"	X	X	X
"out the back door"		X	X
outside of the foot	X	X	
Half volley			
sole of the foot	X	X	X
inside of the foot		X	X
redirecting forward		X	X
"touch and turn"			X
"out the back door"			X
outside of the foot		X	X
Air ball			
inside of the foot		X	X
redirecting forward		X	X
"touch and turn"			X
"out the back door"			X
outside of foot		X	X
instep		X	X

Table 6-1. (*Continued*).

Level of Player* Approximate Age*	Suggested Emphasis		
	Beginning 6–9 yrs.	**Intermediate** 10–13 yrs.	**Advanced** 14 yrs. & up
inside of the thigh		X	X
"touch and turn"			X
top of the thigh		X	X
chest		X	X
"touch and turn"			X
"over the top"			X
head		X	X
redirecting forward			X
"touch and turn"			X
"over the top"			X

*Note that beginning, intermediate, and advanced categories do not always correspond with the age ranges. Coaches should use this classification system as an approximation, adjusting the techniques to suit their players' ability levels. Experimentation with all techniques should be safely encouraged.

7
Dribbling and Maintaining Control

INTRODUCTION

The skill of dribbling involves maneuvering the ball on the ground with different parts of the feet. Mastering the ball is the essence of soccer, which makes learning how to dribble both important and fun. Dribbling has several purposes:

- to advance the ball into scoring position
- to maneuver the ball past an opponent in order to maintain possession
- to maneuver the ball into open space where there is sufficient time in which to pass or shoot
- to maintain possession to give teammates time to get into open space to receive a pass
- to create a numerical advantage in other areas of the field after beating a player or drawing defenders

Dribbling is employed mainly in the middle and attacking third of the field. It is risky for a player to dribble out of the defensive third of the field, because a successful tackle may enable the opponents to score. Beginning players also need to learn that advancing the ball by dribbling is not as quick as passing, as long as teammates are in open positions to receive a pass.

Young players need lots of trial-and-error opportunities to discover how to dribble. Simple practices that promote dribbling in small-sided scrimmages will ensure that players are learning the basics through self-discovery. Encourage players to refine dribbling skills outside scheduled practice sessions. And remember: Let the game teach the kids!

The details and diagrams in this chapter give coaches and parents material for the occasional BRIEF teaching point or demonstration.

FUNDAMENTALS OF DRIBBLING

Three individual dribbling techniques can be used to maneuver the ball on the ground. Regardless of the technique, dribbling involves the fundamentals of control, vision, and rhythm.

Control

The relative ease with which a player maintains possession of the ball when dribbling is a measure of control. When opponents are closely marking a player dribbling the ball, the ball must be maintained near the feet (close control) so that the ball can be quickly maneuvered away from the marking players. When defenders are not marking closely, the ball can be dribbled farther away from the feet.

Vision

Beginning players tend to watch the ball when they dribble, making them vulnerable to unexpected tackles. Good vision in soccer involves viewing both the ball and the setting away from the ball (looking off the ball). Scanning the field is critical to knowing what the options are at all times and making the right decisions, for both offensive and defensive players.

Skilled dribblers maintain an elevated head and neck posture when dribbling. When defenders see a dribbler look off the ball, they may become hesitant in their attempts to tackle. Defenders know that a dribbler who is scanning may be looking for teammates who are open to receive a pass. The dribbler may gain additional time and space as the defender prepares to respond to a pass. Skilled dribblers look off the ball to reduce defensive pressure even when they know their teammates are not open to receive a pass.

Rhythm

Rhythm, associated with all individual dribbling techniques, refers to the ability of a player to naturally move with the ball without substantially interrupting the running pattern. It involves a compatibility between the pace and position of the rolling ball and the speed of the run. Figures 7-1 to 7-3 illustrate three dribbling techniques using the inside of the foot, outside of the foot, and instep.

Figure 7-1. Dribbling with the inside of the foot.

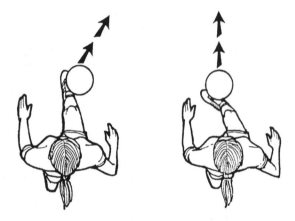

Figure 7-2. Dribbling with the outside of the foot—leg position and direction of ball.

Figure 7-3. Dribbling with the instep.

PROGRESSIONS FOR TEACHING INDIVIDUAL DRIBBLING TECHNIQUES

Each of the three individual dribbling techniques should be taught to beginning players. The following guidelines are helpful in sequencing an approach to teaching these techniques.

- Have players practice the three individual dribbling techniques with both of their feet.
- Select exercises that encourage players to progress from practicing dribbling techniques at a slow pace to practicing these techniques at a fast pace.
- Encourage players to progress from dribbling the ball moderate distances away from their feet to dribbling under close control.
- Challenge players by having them initially practice dribbling in unlimited space, then gradually restrict their practice space.
- Tell dribblers to change speed and direction, while controlling the ball and maintaining vision of the field.

INDIVIDUAL TECHNIQUES TO MAINTAIN CONTROL OF THE DRIBBLE

Dribbling, in its simplest form, involves the use of a combination of the three individual dribbling techniques to move the ball along the ground in a straight path toward an opponent's goal. This approach, however, is not likely to be successful in a game situation in which defenders are marking the dribbler and attempting to tackle the ball away. Thus, the application of dribbling to game conditions must be more creative and include additional techniques to aid players in maintaining control of the ball. Figures 7-4 to 7-16 illustrate these controlling techniques. Note that several involve the use of feints, which are actions taken by a player to deceive an opponent.

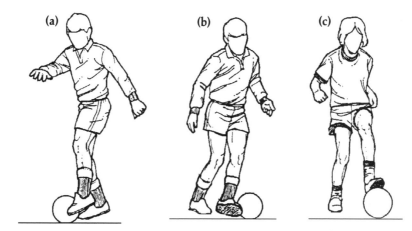

Figure 7-4. Slowing the pace of a rolling ball by (a) hooking the ball with the inside of the instep, (b) hooking the ball with the outside of the instep, and (c) applying pressure with the sole of the foot.

Figure 7-5. Turning the ball with the inside of the foot.

Figure 7-6. Turning the ball with the inside of the foot in front of a defender.

Figure 7-7. Turning the ball with the outside of the foot.

Figure 7-8. Using the sole of the right foot to turn the ball across the front of the body toward the left.

(a) (b)

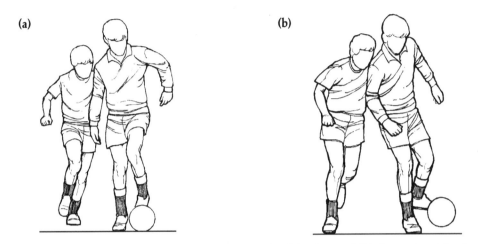

Figure 7-9. Shielding the ball while dribbling with (a) the outside of the foot and (b) the inside of the foot.

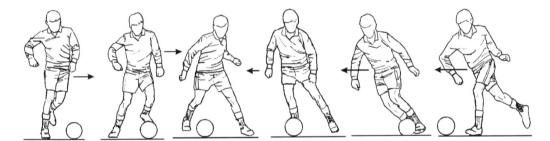

Figure 7-10. Body feint and inside of the foot dribble.

Figure 7-11. Body feint and outside of the foot dribble.

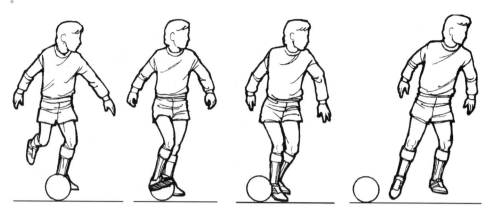

Figure 7-12. Inside-out feint and outside of the foot dribble.

Figure 7-13. Outside-in feint and inside of the foot dribble.

Figure 7-14. Step-over and inside of the foot turn.

PROGRESSIONS FOR TEACHING TECHNIQUES TO MAINTAIN CONTROL OF THE DRIBBLE

It takes years for soccer players to become proficient at dribbling while maintaining control, vision, and rhythm. Coaches should introduce dribbling exercises that do not include defensive pressure initially. As players learn the basics of controlling the ball, coaches should add defensive pressure. Players should also learn body feints before they try ball feints.

Table 7-1 includes a list of dribbling and maintaining control techniques, rated by level of difficulty. Coaches and parents can use it as a general guide to determine a rough sequence in which these skills should be taught. Remember: Let the game teach the kids!

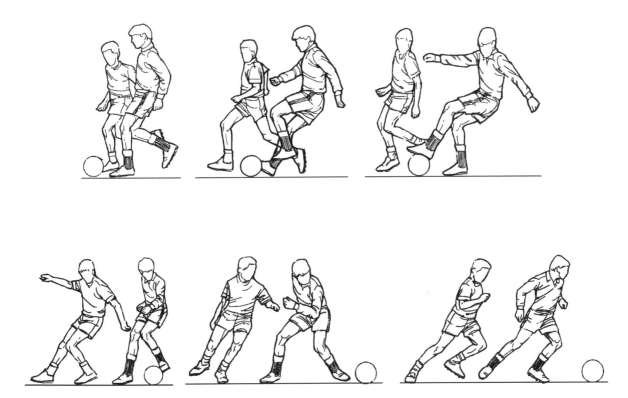

Figure 7-15. Sole of the foot stop and turn.

Figure 7-16. Sole of the foot stop and go.

Table 7-1. Dribbling and Maintaining Control—Difficulty Rating Form.

Level of Player* Approximate Age*	Suggested Emphasis		
	Beginning 6–9 yrs.	**Intermediate** 10–13 yrs.	**Advanced** 14 yrs. & up
Individual Techniques			
Dribbling			
inside of the foot	X	X	X
outside of the foot	X	X	X
instep	X	X	X
Maintaining Control			
slowing the pace			
hooking the ball with the inside of the instep	X	X	X
hooking the ball with the outside of the instep	X	X	X
applying pressure to the top of the ball with the sole of the foot	X	X	X
increasing the pace			
inside of the foot	X	X	X
outside of the foot	X	X	X
instep	X	X	X
changing direction (turning the ball)			
inside of the foot	X	X	X
outside of the foot	X	X	X
sole of the foot	X	X	X
shielding			
inside of the foot	X	X	X
outside of the foot	X	X	X
Feinting			
body feints		X	X
ball feints			X
body and ball feints			X

*Note that beginning, intermediate, and advanced categories do not always correspond with the age ranges. Coaches should use this classification system as an approximation, adjusting the techniques to suit their players' ability levels.

8
Heading

INTRODUCTION

The technique of heading involves the use of the head to pass, shoot, or receive a soccer ball. Specifically, the head may be used to clear a high cross, advance the ball to a teammate, receive a high pass, or deflect a lofted ball into the goal.

The importance of heading in the game of soccer varies with the nature of play and the age (or ability) of the players. Heading skills are important in games involving intermediate and advanced youth players who can make accurate air ball passes.

DEVELOPMENTAL CONCERNS

Four factors should be considered before encouraging young athletes to strike the ball with the head.

Ball Impact Force

The impact force in heading is determined from the weight of the ball and the speed at which it approaches the head. The impact force can be very large because of high ball speeds.

Neck Muscle Strength

The muscles of the neck, which are important in heading, are relatively weak in athletes under 12 years of age. As a consequence, they will often align the head, neck, and trunk with the path of the approaching ball in order to absorb the impact force in line with the body, and to prevent possible injury. By comparison, the adult player will properly receive this force more perpendicular to the line of the head, neck, and trunk.

Control of Head Movements

Relatively weak muscles of the neck and incomplete motor development in young athletes may result in improper forehead contact with the ball. Contacting the ball with regions of the head other than the forehead may increase chances of injury.

Development of the Spine

The bones (vertebrae) that compose the spine do not fully develop until 25 to 30 years of age. Potential impact forces from heading may be injurious to the neck (cervical) vertebrae of young soccer players. Therefore, any form of heading should not be practiced in games or scrimmages by players under 8 years of age. With the use of softer balls or beach balls, proper fundamental techniques can be introduced to young players. They should know the proper basic techniques of heading long before they use the skill in practices or games.

FUNDAMENTALS OF HEADING

Body Position and Movement

Prior to heading a ball, the trunk should be arched back (Figure 8-1). This movement will result in a noticeable tension in the stomach

Figure 8-1. Sequence of movement in heading.

muscles and will aid in the subsequent vigorous forward bending movement of the trunk that follows.

Arm Position and Movement

During the preparatory phase of heading, the arms are held forward and bent slightly at the elbows. This will assist in lateral balance. As the forward bending movement of the trunk occurs, the player may forcefully draw arms back. This movement of the arms assists the trunk's forward movement and the resultant impact velocity of the head to the ball.

Method of Contact

Contact with the ball should be made with the forehead (Figure 8-2). This generally flat region of the head permits good ball control. The frontal bone of the skull, which encompasses the forehead, is also relatively thick and strong. The eyes should be open and focused on the ball to insure that contact is made with the forehead.

Heading the ball in regions other than the forehead may be painful and injurious and should be avoided. The player can accelerate the forward speed of the head by simultaneously flexing the neck as the forehead is extended into the ball. When contact occurs, the jaw should be held firmly in place with the mouth closed and the tongue retracted. The muscles of the neck should be tightened to prevent the head from recoiling. Figures 8-3 and 8-4 illustrate additional points about heading a soccer ball.

Figure 8-2. Forehead contact with the ball.

Figure 8-3. Orientation of forehead and path of the ball.

Figure 8-4. Sequence of movement in jumping to head ball forward from a two-foot takeoff.

RECOMMENDED PROGRESSIONS FOR TEACHING HEADING

If coaches select teaching methods, practice techniques and equipment that are commensurate with the physical development of their young athletes, heading skills can be introduced.

Table 8-1 contains a suggested progression for teaching heading skills. Each coach, however, must assume the responsibility of determining, in all cases, whether or not individual players can safely perform each step in the progression. Table 8-2 rates the difficulty of heading techniques.

Table 8-1. Progression for Teaching Heading

Age (Years)	Focus of Activity and Instruction	Comments and Concerns
Under 8	Not Recommended	Heading is not recommended because of relatively weak neck musculature and lack of control of movement of the head.
8-9	1. Teach proper body positioning and movement. 2. Instruct players to hold a ball against the forehead while they assume the proper feet and body position with eyes open. 3. Allow players to lightly bounce a soft ball off the forehead.	Allowing the player to control light bounces off the forehead permits self-regulation and reduces fear. At most, 20 minutes of practice time in a 10-week session should be allotted for heading practice, with a soft ball. Emphasis on other skills such as dribbling, kicking, and receiving is more important at this age.

Table 8-1 *(Continued)*

Age (Years)	Focus of Activity and Instruction	Comments and Concerns
10-11	1. Instruct players to toss, head, and catch a ball themselves. Vary the exercises by either having them receive and control the headed ball or head the ball to a teammate positioned three to five yards away. 2. Teach players to juggle the ball with the head. 3. Initiate heading exercises in which underhand tosses, using two hands, are made to a partner. 4. Use heading exercises which challenge players by requiring them to: move to head the ball, head to a moving target, or head the ball in different directions.	Continue using exercises in which players have self-control over heading impact forces. However, a transition should be made to heading balls tossed by a partner standing up to five yards away. The coach must continually monitor tosses for excessive height, distance, and spin on the ball. Approximately five minutes of every other practice is appropriate for work on heading skills with this age group.
12-13	1. Allow players to toss a ball 10 to 20 feet to a partner who returns the ball with a head pass. 2. Players should be taught how to jump and head. 3. Players should be taught how to receive a ball with the head.	Heading becomes a more important part of the game at this age. Most players have sufficient neck strength and control of head movements to head tossed balls. Additional heading skills, such as jumping to head the ball and receiving, should be taught. As much as five minutes per practice session could be spent in practicing heading skills through the use of a variety of exercises.
14 and above	1. Permit players to pratice heading balls which are thrown or kicked 20 to 40 feet. 2. All heading techniques should be taught.	Most players will be mature enough to head balls which are kicked to them. They should be able to execute variations of heading skills from a standing and airborne position.

Table 8-2. Heading—Difficulty Rating Form.

Level of Player* Approximate Age*	Suggested Emphasis		
	Beginning 6–9 yrs.	Intermediate 10–13 yrs.	Advanced 14 yrs. & up
Individual Techniques			
Heading while on the ground			
forward heading		X	X
sideward heading		X	X
backward heading		X	X
Heading while in the air			
jump heading forward		X	X
jump heading sideward			X
jump heading backward			X
dive heading			X

*Note that beginning, intermediate, and advanced categories do not always correspond with the age ranges. Coaches should use this classification system as an approximation, adjusting the techniques to suit their players' ability levels.

**Heading is not recommended for players under eight years of age, regardless of the ability of the player.

9
Throw-In

INTRODUCTION

The throw-in is an essential part of the game of soccer. It is the method by which the ball is put back into play after it goes out of bounds over the touch line (side line). Youth soccer players must not be put into game competition without knowing this important skill.

The team in possession of the ball for the throw-in has the advantage if its players are able to quickly and accurately put the ball into play. A properly thrown ball is as effective as a well-executed pass.

RULES OF PLAY GOVERNING THE THROW-IN

The rules of play restrict the variability in technique used for the throw-in. They define the location and method for the throw-in.

Location

The throw-in must occur at the point where the ball went out of bounds. The throw-in must be taken with both feet on the ground, either on the touch line or outside the touch line (Figure 9-1). In an illegal throw-in, one or both of the feet are completely over the touch line in the field of play. If one foot is off the ground, this is also an illegal throw-in (Figure 9-2).

Figure 9-1. Legal foot placement during the throw-in.

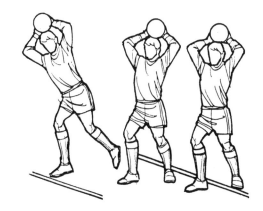

Figure 9-2. Illegal foot placement during the throw-in.

Method

1. The thrower must face the field of play.
2. Both feet must be in contact with the ground when the ball leaves the hands.
3. The throw-in is made with a two-handed throw, in which each hand must apply approximately equal force to the ball.
4. The throw-in must consist of one continuous movement in which the ball is taken from behind the head and released over the head.

Even with these restricting rules, considerable variability in technique is possible in this important skill. Figures 9-3 through 9-7 illustrate leg, foot, and hand positions in the throw-in, as well as movement sequences.

Figure 9-3. Side Straddle.

Figure 9-4. Forward-backward straddle.

Figure 9-5. Hand position.

Figure 9-6. Sequential movement in the stationary throw-in.

Figure 9-7. Sequence of movement in the approach run and throw-in.

Beginning soccer players will probably make predictable mistakes as they learn throw-in techniques. Table 9-1 identifies several common errors and methods for correcting them. Table 9-2 lists throw-in techniques, rated by level of difficulty. Coaches and parents can use it as a general guide to determine a rough sequence in which these skills should be taught. Remember: let the game teach the kids!

Table 9-1. Technique errors in taking the throw-in.

Throw-in Error	Probable Correction
Unequal force applied to the ball by the hands during the throw	A top-like spin imparted to the ball is usually caused when the player throws the ball from the dominant hand side of the head. It can be corrected by having the player concentrate on bringing the ball forward directly over the middle of the head and attempting to throw with a little lateral spin.
Lifting the back foot in the forward-backward (diagonal) straddle during the throw	If the player is using a stationary throw-in, the body weight should be positioned more toward the back foot. If a running approach is used, the player should take a longer straddle step following the hop to keep the body position in back of the front foot.
Falling off balance when using a side straddle	Little forward-backward stability is provided by a side straddle. The player should switch to a diagonal straddle.
Stepping beyond the touch line	Player should practice throw-ins with a restraining line to understand how to confine the approach run.
Failure to bring the ball behind the head	The player should remember to "touch" the back of the neck with the ball.

Table 9-2. Throw-in—Difficulty Rating Form.

	Suggested Emphasis		
Level of Player* **Approximate Age***	**Beginning** 6–9 yrs.	**Intermediate** 10–13 yrs.	**Advanced** 14 yrs. & up
Individual Techniques			
Stationary throw-in			
side straddle	X		
forward-backward straddle	X	X	
Approach run and throw-in	X	X	X

*Note that beginning, intermediate, and advanced categories do not always correspond with the age ranges. Coaches should use this classification system as an approximation, adjusting the techniques to suit their players' ability levels.

10
Defensive Techniques

INTRODUCTION

Players use individual defensive techniques for three basic purposes:

- to regain possession of the ball
- to decrease the potential for the offensive team to maintain possession of the ball
- to decrease the potential for the offensive team to score a goal

Young players need lots of trial-and-error opportunities to learn defensive techniques. Small-sided scrimmages will ensure that players are learning the basics through self-discovery. Encourage players to refine defensive skills outside scheduled practice sessions. And remember: Let the game teach the kids!

The details and diagrams in this chapter give coaches and parents material for the occasional BRIEF teaching point or demonstration.

FUNDAMENTAL DEFENSIVE PRINCIPLE

Marking and tackling are the individual defensive techniques. They are used in both zone and player-to-player defenses. All players must be taught how to mark and tackle. However, in order for these individual techniques to be effective, the fundamental defensive principle must be applied: *all players defend immediately upon loss of possession.*

INDIVIDUAL TECHNIQUES

Marking

In marking, the defender is positioned near and on the defensive goal side of an opponent. There are two types of marking: marking a player in possession of the ball and marking a player who does not have possession of the ball (Figures 10-1 and 10-2).

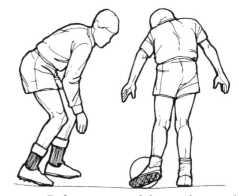

Figure 10-1. Body position and focus when marking a player in possession of the ball.

Figure 10-2. Body position and focus when marking a player who does not have possession of the ball.

Tackling

Tackling is the act of taking a ball directly from an opponent, using one of several techniques. The type of tackle to be performed depends upon the relative position and direction of movement of the offensive and defensive players. Individual tackling techniques are described in Figures 10-3 through 10-10.

Smart coaches understand that defensive techniques are an integral part of the game of soccer. Their practices include time for demonstration and scrimmages so their players learn how to execute defensive moves effectively.

Figure 10-3. Front block tackle.

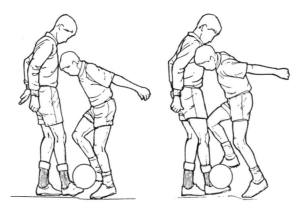

Figure 10-4. Front block tackle and scoop.

Figure 10-5. Front block tackle and push between the legs.

Figure 10-6. Front block tackle and draw back.

Figure 10-7. Pivot tackle.

Figure 10-8. Toe poke.

Figure 10-9. Bent leg slide tackle.

Figure 10-10. Hook slide tackle.

Table 10-1 includes a list of defensive techniques, rated by level of difficulty. Coaches and parents can use it as a general guide to determine a rough sequence in which these skills should be taught. Remember: Let the game teach the kids!

Table 10-1. Defensive Techniques—Difficulty Rating Form.

Level of Player* Approximate Age*	Suggested Emphasis		
	Beginning 6–9 yrs.	Intermediate 10–13 yrs.	Advanced 14 yrs. & up
Individual Techniques			
Marking			
player in possession of the ball	X	X	X
player not in possession of the ball	X	X	X
Tackling			
front block tackle	X	X	X
pivot tackle		X	X
side tackle	X	X	X
slide tackle			
bent leg			X
hook			X

*Note that beginning, intermediate, and advanced categories do not always correspond with the age ranges given beneath it. Coaches should use this classification system as an approximation, adjusting the techniques to suit their players' ability levels.

11
Goalkeeping

INTRODUCTION

The goalkeeper (goalie or keeper) is the last line of defense in preventing balls from entering the goal and the first line of attack in initiating offensive play after a save. The keeper is the only member of a soccer team who can legally use the hands to control the ball, but only within the goalkeeper's own penalty area.

Players on a youth soccer team should take turns at the goalkeeper position during practices. Young players need lots of trial-and-error opportunities to learn the skills for this crucial role. Small-sided scrimmages will ensure that players are learning the basics through self-discovery. For games, coaches are likely to select goalkeepers on the basis of above average stature, agility, courage, confidence, quickness, strength, and decisiveness, particularly during the early part of the season. Goalkeepers are best switched at halftime and quarter breaks in youth competition. Remember: let the game teach the kids!

The details and diagrams in this chapter give coaches and parents material for the occasional BRIEF teaching point or demonstration.

FUNDAMENTALS OF GOALKEEPING

Ready Position (Starting Position)

When the opponents have the ball close to the goalkeeper's goal, the goalkeeper should be in a ready position (Figure 11-1). The goalkeeper should be mentally and physically alert. In the ready position, the knees and trunk are bent and the feet are approximately shoulder-width apart with weight forward on the balls of the feet. The arms are spread at waist height. The hands should be out in front, elbows bent, fingers up and palms out, about waist high. The hands and arms supply the additional springing momentum not provided by the legs. The eyes are fixed on the ball, with concentration extended to players around the penalty area.

Figure 11-1. Ready Position.

The purpose of the ready position is to allow the keeper to be able to move quickly, yet remain comfortable and relaxed so that the mind can be focused on the game. When there is no immediate threat on goal, a goalkeeper can maintain a moderate level of attention by jogging in place or moving around the penalty area near the arc.

To recap, the key elements are:

- positioning the feet shoulder-width apart
- bending the knees and trunk slightly
- distributing the body weight forward and onto the balls of the feet
- positioning the hands in front of the body
- keeping mentally alert.

Common errors include:

- positioning feet too far apart, resulting in delayed body movement
- positioning feet too close together, resulting in instability
- carrying hands at sides or placing them on the knees instead of in front of the body, resulting in delayed reaction
- not concentrating on the ball and opposing players.

Positioning

Other than during set plays, such as a penalty kick or a free kick, the goalkeeper should not be in a stationary position. When the ball is in motion, the keeper is in motion. A goalkeeper must change positions in the goal area by reacting to the play. Positioning is three-dimensional: left, right, and overhead. The first priority is to protect the near post.

A goalkeeper should move along an imaginary arc (Figure 11-2) that decreases the opening to the goal for the player with the ball and also provides the best positioning to stop a shot on goal. This position is along an imaginary line that connects the ball and the center of the goal line. Before play, it is advisable for goalkeepers to create a mark, with their cleats, at the center of the goal line to use as a guide for proper positioning. As the ball approaches the goal, the imaginary arc should get closer to the goal. Note, if the ball is along the goal line and away from the goal (in a poor shooting position), the goalkeeper should retreat toward the far post. However, if the ball is brought toward the goal from the wing into a shooting position, the goalkeeper must come to the near post.

One of the best aids in helping young keepers visualize correct angle play is a rope. Tie one end to the post and stretch it out to

where the ball lies. The rope now delineates the widest possible ball paths. As the ball moves, so does the rope. Utilizing the rope and the goal line, you have created a triangle. The ball should always be directly in the center of the goalkeeper, thus creating "the ball line."

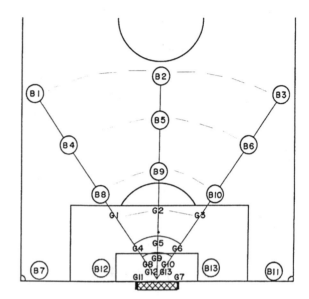

Figure 11-2. Goalkeeper positioning in response to ball position. The letters "B" and "G" with the same numbers designate corresponding pairs of ball positions and goalkeeper positions.

To be correctly positioned, a goalkeeper must face the ball. In most situations, movement sideways should involve small shuffle steps in which the feet do not cross one another so the goalkeeper can quickly transfer the body weight from one foot to the other. If a goalkeeper rests on one foot or hops, it may be hard to change direction rapidly.

If the ball is struck with power, the goalkeeper must apply the crossover footwork. This enables the keeper to generate more speed than the sideways shuffle. Should the keeper need to move quickly to the left, the right leg crosses the left leg. The reverse is true to the opposite direction. Regardless of the use of a sideways shuffle or crossover, the keeper needs to be balanced to make the save.

To recap, the key elements of effective positioning include:

- using an imaginary arc
- facing the ball

- using short and quick shuffle steps
- keeping body weight forward onto the balls of the feet

Common errors include:

- moving too far off the goal line
- remaining on the goal line
- hopping sideways
- crossing the legs
- standing flat footed, with weight primarily on the heels

One of the first techniques youth soccer players should be taught about playing goalkeeper is how to correctly position themselves around the goal. Goalkeepers should be taught to:

1. position themselves correctly in response to each of several balls located outside and inside the penalty area;
2. continually assume proper positioning in response to the changing location of a ball that is dribbled outside and inside the penalty area;
3. continually assume proper positioning in response to movements of a player dribbling, stopping, changing directions, and faking shots;
4. assume proper positions in response to players taking shots on goal from stationary positions to the left, center, and right of the goal; and
5. assume proper positions in response to attacking players receiving and shooting balls served to the left, center, and right of the goal.

Narrowing the Angle on a Breakaway

When an offensive player with the ball is unmarked and has an open path to the goal without the chance of being marked by a defender, the goalkeeper should move into a position to maximize the possibility of making a save. The goalkeeper should quickly advance, under control, along an imaginary line from the center of the goal line to the ball. This line bisects the shooting angle (Figure 11-3). The goalkeeper should have the arms out to the sides to reduce the visually open area of the

goal. As the goalkeeper advances in a balanced and controlled manner, the target area for the attacking player becomes smaller.

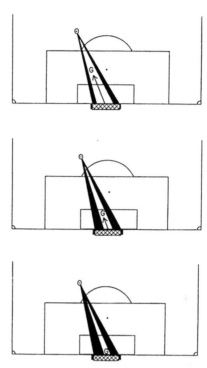

Figure 11-3. Narrowing the angle. As the goalkeeper moves closer to the ball, the area of the goal that appears to be visually open, narrows, or decreases.

The order of desirable outcomes (from most desirable to least) that the goalkeeper should attempt to achieve in stopping a breakaway is:

1. Get the ball before the attacker shoots.
2. Get to the ball as the shot is being taken.
3. Block the ball immediately after the shot is taken.

If the goalkeeper gets to the ball before the attacker, the goalkeeper can catch or dive and catch the ball in a variety of ways. However, if the goalkeeper arrives simultaneously as the shot is being taken, or slightly after the shot, the goalkeeper must quickly react by diving to the side of the intended shot. This is potentially dangerous, so goalkeepers must be taught how to protect themselves. Basically, a dive is made to position the goalkeeper in front of the attacker. The top arm must be positioned away from and in front of the face (Figure 11-4). This positioning of the top arm is used to:

- permit a good view of the actions of the shooter
- absorb the blow of a kick toward the face and head
- enable the goalkeeper to react and protect the trunk
- aid in blocking or catching the shot.

Figure 11-4. Body and arm position when landing, after the dive, in front of the kicker.

When properly diving in front of an attacking player, the objective of the goalkeeper is to block the ball with the arms, body, or legs. The goalkeeper's stomach may be the most vulnerable body part. Therefore, strong abdominal muscles are important.

When executing a breakaway save, the hands should always be on the inside of the goalpost. Three reasons why:

- The keeper can push the ball away from the goal, to avoid deflecting the ball to the center of the field.
- When the keeper reloads, the hands are anchored back into the goal for a solid position.
- The keeper can use the feet as a second set of hands.

To recap, the key elements are:

- Visualize a shooting angle. (Note, this can be practiced by connecting string from the ball to the goal posts.)
- Bisect the shooting angle.
- Move along the imaginary line quickly and under control.
- Before the shot is taken, momentarily assume a ready position.
- Present as big a barrier as long as possible.

Common errors include:

- giving the attacking player a larger target area on one side of the goal

- staying on the goal line and not coming out to approach the ball
- approaching the ball without maintaining controlled body movements
- advancing too slowly or too quickly (Movements of the keeper reflect the speed of the ball, player, and additionally the angle of approach.)
- running out from the goal to play an attacker who is being marked by a defender
- not having the hands and arms extended toward the near post side.

If goalkeepers are taught how and when to come out from the goal line in order to narrow the shooting angle of an attacking player, they will not feel as threatened in this potentially dangerous event. The closer the ball gets to the keeper, the lower the keeper gets. From close range, the keeper is vulnerable to low shots. Goalkeepers should be taught to:

1. assume a proper positioning of the top arm while on the ground,
2. approach a ball placed on the ground and go down as if to make a save,
3. approach and stop a shot from an attacking player who has been instructed to kick softly at the ball, and
4. approach an attacking player, who is being pursued from behind by a defender, and attempt to stop the shot on goal (realistic breakaway).

Supporting the Defense

The goalkeeper must support teammates at all times through correct positioning and effective communication with the defense.

The goalkeeper is in an ideal position to assume or be assigned the responsibility of communicating with the defense (directing the defense) because play is usually visible over the entire field. The goalkeeper should communicate in a loud and clear voice to prevent mistakes, misunderstandings, and lapses in concentration. A goalkeeper can tell teammates to "cover" or "mark" opponents, "pressure" a player with the ball, "shift" position on the field, and give a "support pass" back to the goalkeeper. By yelling "keeper" or "goalie" the goalkeeper is telling teammates not to play the ball, because the goalkeeper is in a better position to take charge of play.

Communication must be given as early as possible so defenders have sufficient time to respond. On the other hand, when a defender has good control of the ball and is not under immediate pressure, it is not appropriate for a goalkeeper to shout extraneous information, because this may unsettle the defender. Key elements in effective goalkeeper communication are listed below.

- Communicate with authority in a loud and clear voice.
- Instill confidence by communicating correct information.
- Communicate with short phrases and key words.
- Anticipate and communicate early.

Coaches and parents should:

1. Establish a list of key words and short commands and review their meanings with all players.
2. Have the goalkeeper shout appropriate information to unopposed defenders as a ball is kicked into the penalty area.

3. Have the goalkeeper direct three or more defenders against three or more attacking players.
4. Have the goalkeeper direct the defense in full-sided games.
5. Have the goalkeeper direct the defense in various restarts.

Shot Stopping

Each shot on goal requires the goalkeeper to engage in a quick decision-making process.

First, the goalkeeper must judge the level of difficulty in stopping the shot. Table 11-1 presents several factors that influence the level of difficulty. These factors can be manipulated by a coach to create challenges for goalkeepers in practice.

Second, the goalkeeper must decide whether to attempt to catch the ball or to punch or deflect it away from the goal. For shots that are relatively easy to stop, the goalkeeper should attempt to catch. Shots that are relatively difficult to stop should be punched or deflected.

Table 11-1. Factors influencing the level of difficulty in stopping shots on goal.

		Factors					
Level of Difficulty	Conditions of Play	Pressure	Pace of the Ball	Weather Conditions	Point of the Kick	Location of Shot on Goal	Technique Selection
Relatively easy	Practice-like	No pressure from attacking players	Slow	Calm, dry	Far from the goal	Close to the goalkeeper	Preselected by coach or goalkeeper based on predetermined path and pace of ball
Moderate		Passive pressure from attacking players	Intermediate		Intermediate distance		
Relatively difficult	Game-like	Pressure from attacking players	Fast	Windy, wet	Close to the goal	Away from the goalkeeper	Selection made by goalkeeper based on conditions of play at the time of the shot

Catching. Goalkeepers use two basic forms of catching: underhand (scoop) and overhand catching (Figures 11-5 and 11-6). Underhand catching is used on ball received below the chest (Figures 11-7 to 11-9). Overhand catching is used on balls received above the chest (Figures 11-10 to 11-12).

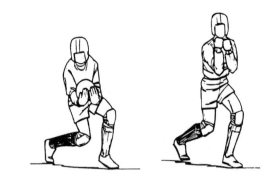

Figure 11-8. Waist-high air ball scoop catch.

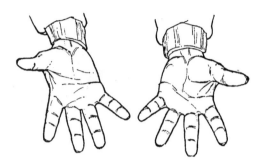

Figure 11-5. Hand positioning for underhand catching.

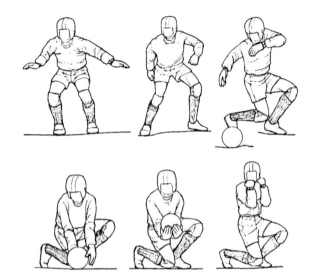

Figure 11-9. Kneeling scoop catch.

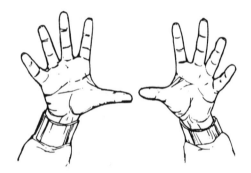

Figure 11-6. Hand positioning for overhand catching.

Figure 11-7. Standing scoop catch.

Figure 11-10. Chest-high overhand catch.

Figure 11-11. Above-head catch on a ball with a steep arc.

Figure 11-12. Above-head jump and catch.

It is possible to use either form of catching from the chest region. Generally, if the ball is received at the chest from a relatively steep arc, it should be caught in an underhand position. Fast-moving balls with shallow trajectories should be received at the chest with overhand positioning.

Catching by a goalkeeper primarily involves the use of the fingers and palms of both hands to reduce the speed of the ball so that it can be controlled. For all catching in soccer, this process consists of four elements: positioning, reaching, controlling, and securing.

- **Positioning:** From the ready position, the goalkeeper must move in line with the path of the ball. Positioning the body in this manner allows the goalkeeper to use various body parts as a second barrier behind the hands. If

sufficient time is not available to position the body in line with the path of the ball, the goalkeeper should attempt to get as close as possible to reduce the difficulty in catching the ball. One of the first techniques youth players should be taught about playing goalkeeper is how to position themselves correctly in goal. Moving to position may involve footwork and/or diving.

- **Reaching:** The second element of catching involves projecting the hands toward the ball and using the elbows as shock absorbers. This action positions the hands close together and in line with the approaching ball to form an initial barrier in its path. A full reach should be achieved before the ball contacts the hands.
- **Controlling:** When the ball contacts the hands, they should be drawn back to reduce

the pace of the ball. Control is enhanced if the hands contact the ball over a broad area (i.e., fingers spread) and if the pace of the ball is reduced over a relatively long period of time (i.e., drawing the hands back while in contact with the ball).

- **Securing:** Once the pace of the ball has been reduced, it should not be left exposed to attacking players. This could entice attackers to kick at the ball and endanger the goalkeeper.

The goalkeeper should secure a ball caught from a standing or kneeling position by wrapping the hands and arms around it with the elbows close together (Figure 11-13).

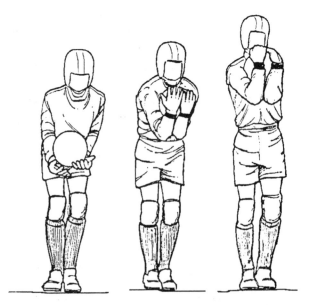

Figure 11-13. Securing the ball with the hands and arms.

A ball controlled while the goalkeeper is on the ground should be drawn into the trunk with the arms wrapped around the ball. The top leg should be swung forward to protect the ball and goalkeeper from late kicks (Figure 11-14). This positioning also gives the goalkeeper a view of the field of play and an opportunity to decide upon which distribution technique to use.

Figure 11-14. Securing the ball while on the ground.

Punching and Deflecting: If the goalkeeper is uncertain that a shot on goal can be caught, then the ball should be punched or deflected away from the goal. Attempting to catch a ball that is beyond the goalkeeper's ability to do so is a typical error made by youth players. If the ball is missed, it may proceed into the goal or rebound in front of the goal where an attacking player can take another shot. By punching or deflecting a shot, the goalkeeper is preventing a goal, acquiring additional time to react to subsequent play, and providing time for the defense to reorganize.

When punching a ball, the goalkeeper should attempt to project the ball far out of the penalty area and to the side of the goal. The goalkeeper should attempt to punch the ball with the knuckles of both fists to achieve height, width, and distance (Figure 11-15). However, when diving to stop a ball shot to the top or bottom corners of the goal, the goalkeeper can gain additional reach by using one hand.

Figure 11-15. Using both fists in punching.

The keeper should utilize a two-fisted punch to send the ball back to where it came from. It is usually performed on frontal serves. The one-fisted punch is utilized to change the flight of the ball, i.e., from left to right.

Deflecting involves the use of the heels of the hands and fingers to redirect the ball. The keeper should lock the wrist for safety and power. As in punching, the goalkeeper should be taught to use two hands whenever possible. A deflection should be used when it is difficult for the goalkeeper to punch the ball sufficiently far from the goal. Deflections are used to redirect the ball: a) in bounds to either side of the goal where the angle for shooting is difficult; b) out of bounds to either side of the goal, giving up a corner kick; c) out of bounds over the goal post, giving up a corner kick; or d) to deflect over the cross bar.

Diving

A dive is used to quickly position the body to play a ball, which is relatively far from the goalkeeper, when sufficient time is not available to run to position. Through the use of good positioning, the goalkeeper minimizes the number of times he/she is called upon to have to dive to make a save. However, the goalkeeper must be ready at all times to respond by diving in an attempt to stop a shot on goal.

Components of a Good Save: There are five components of a diving save: takeoff, flight, save, landing, and cover-up.

• **Takeoff:** The takeoff is initiated from a ready position. As foot to the side of the intended dive is listed, the opposite foot pushes the body to the side so a short side step is quickly taken onto the lifted foot (Figure 11-16). Throughout this movement the trunk must maintain a position facing the field of play, the arms are swung back, and the body should be lowered. From this position, the leading leg is forcefully extended while the trailing leg is lifted. This has been called the power step. Simultaneous with the action of the legs, the arms are forcefully swung over the head. The leg and arm movements drive the body into the air.

Figure 11-16. Diving—takeoff and flight.

- **Flight:** The flight is the path of the body in the air. The path taken must be compatible with the location of the ball. The path, however, is determined at takeoff by the action of the legs and arms. Regardless of the location of the ball, the body must maintain a position with its shoulders, trunk, and hips parallel to the plane of the goal line.
- **Save:** While in the air, the goalkeeper attempts to catch, punch, or deflect the ball.
- **Landing:** A safe landing is accomplished by distributing the blow over a broad area of the body and absorbing the force of landing over a relatively long period of time. The goalkeeper must sequentially contact the ground with segments of the side of the body. For dives used in saving rolling or low air balls, contact with the ground is sequentially made by the outside of the leg, hip, side of the trunk, shoulder, and finally the arm (Figure 11-17). An opposite sequence of contact with the ground is used to absorb the shock of landing from a medium-high to high air ball diving save.

If the ball is caught, it is important for the goalkeeper to maintain possession of the ball. The shock of landing, however, may jar the ball from the goalkeeper's hands. The goalkeeper could use the ball to help absorb some of the shock in landing after a dive to catch medium and high air balls. Only the body should be used to absorb the force of landing when the keeper dives to catch a low shot on goal. This type of dive does not result in as great a lateral shock to the body as that experienced in the dive for a high ball.

Cover-Up

When a ball is caught during a diving save and attacking players are near, the ball should be covered up. Covering the ball serves two functions. If properly performed, it protects the goalkeeper against foul kicks from attacking players and it secures and removes the ball from attackers tempted to kick at what might appear to be a loose ball.

The ball is covered up by bringing it into the stomach. As the ball is secured in the midsection of the body, the arms wrap around the ball and the hips flex (Figure 11-8). The top leg is swung over the bottom leg, further hiding the ball and also forming a barrier to protect the body from errant kicks. The cover-up position permits the goalkeeper to see the field of play and to think about now to distribute the ball.

Key elements of a proper cover-up include:

- starting the dive from a ready position
- taking a short and quick sidestep in the direction of the shot
- driving off the lead leg and quickly swing the trailing leg and arms upward
- facing the field of play throughout the dive
- sequentially absorbing the shock of landing with the ball by rolling out of the dive
- covering up the ball when opponents are near.

Common errors in cover-ups include:

- not being ready to dive
- taking a long sidestep with the foot pointed toward the goal post
- taking a face down ("Superman") dive
- landing on the back
- abruptly absorbing force on landing
- exposing a caught ball to onrushing attackers

When teaching the fundamentals of diving, coaches must avoid exposing goalkeepers to potentially painful experiences. The field should be soft and void of exposed rocks and the grass relatively tall. Coaches or parents may want to water the training area to soften the ground. If available, gymnastic-type mats and high-jump pits are a great help. Goalkeepers should also wear extra clothing and padding (e.g., knee and elbow pads) to practice sessions.

Figure 11-17. Landing sequence from a diving save on a rolling or low air ball.

A progression for teaching the dive involves the following sequence of activities over several training sessions. Goalkeepers should learn how to:

1. Form a "C" curve with the trunk, alternately to the left and right, while in a kneeling position (Figure 11-18). Note that the buttocks should not be resting on the heels and the arms should be extended over the head.

Figure 11-18. "C" curve right with the trunk while kneeling and falling.

2. Fall from a kneeling "C" curve position, alternately to the left and right, and sequentially absorb the force of landing along the side of the body. Goalkeepers should pretend their bodies are like the rockers of a rocking chair to master the sequencing of their falls.
3. Fall from a kneeling "C" curve position and receive and cover up balls alternately rolled to the left and right.
4. Fall, alternately to the left and right, from a squatting position and sequentially absorb the force of landing along the side of the body (Figure 11-19).

5. Fall from a squatting position and receive and cover up balls alternately rolled to the left and right.
6. Take short dives, from a squatting position, to receive and cover up balls alternately rolled to the left and right.
7. Fall from a standing "C" curve position, alternately to the left and right, and sequentially absorb the force of landing along the side of the body.
8. Fall from a standing "C" curve position and receive and cover up balls alternately rolled to the left and right.
9. Take short dives, from a ready position, to receive and cover up balls alternately rolled to the left and right.
10. Take dives of short to intermediate length, from a squatting position, to grasp and cover up balls alternately held low to the left and right.
11. Take dives of short to intermediate length, from a ready position, to grasp and cover up balls alternately held low to the left and right.
12. Practice dives to catch and cover up, punch, and deflect balls kicked at various paces and heights.

Goalkeepers may be called on to roll, throw, punt, or kick the ball from the goal area. Techniques are illustrated in Figures 11-20 to 11-24.

Table 11-2 lists goalkeeping fundamentals and techniques, rated by level of difficulty. Coaches and parents can use it as a general guide to determine a rough sequence in which skills should be taught. Remember: let the game teach the kids!

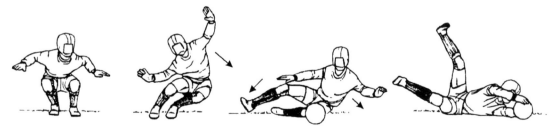

Figure 11-19. Falling from a squatting position.

Figure 11-20. Bowled ball.

Figure 11-21. Sling throw or overhand throw with cross-over step.

Figure 11-22. Baseball throw.

Figure 11-23. Punt from a straight approach.

Figure 11-24. Drop kick with angled approach.

Table 11-2. Goalkeeping—Difficulty Rating Form.

Level of Player* Approximate Age*	Suggested Emphasis		
	Beginning 6–9 yrs.	Intermediate 10–13 yrs.	Advanced 14 yrs. & up
Fundamentals of Goalkeeping			
Ready position	X	X	X
Positioning	X	X	X
Narrowing the Angle on a Breakaway	X	X	X
Supporting the Defense	X	X	X
Shot Stopping			
catching	X	X	X
punching and deflecting	X	X	X
Diving (see Diving Saves)			
Individual Techniques			
Distribution			
bowled ball	X	X	X
sling throw	X	X	X
baseball throw		X	X
punt	X	X	X
drop kick		X	X
goal kick	X	X	X
Saves (catches, punches, and deflections)			
Scoop saves			
standing	X	X	X
low air ball	X	X	X
waist high air ball	X	X	X
chest high air ball	X	X	X
kneeling	X	X	X
half-kneeling	X	X	X
Overhand saves			
chest high	X	X	X
head high	X	X	X
above head	X	X	X
jump save		X	X
Diving saves			
rolling ball	X	X	X
low air ball		X	X
medium-high air ball		X	X
high air ball			X
forward diving			X
back diving punch or deflection			X
drop dive		X	X

*Note that beginning, intermediate, and advanced categories do not always correspond with the age ranges given beneath them. Coaches should use this classification system as an approximation, adjusting the techniques to suit their players' ability levels.

Key to Symbols
Used in Chapter 12 Tactics of Play

O   Offensive player

⊙   Offensive player with ball

O ●   Offensive player taking a restart

X   Defensive player

X⊣   Defensive player marking an opponent

xxxx   Defensive wall of 4 players

Δ   Cone (Pylon)

———→   Direction of player's movement

— — —→   Direction of kicked ball (pass or shot)

⌇⌇⌇→   Direction of player's movement while dribbling the ball

⊗   Coach

ORDER OF EVENTS

1   First Event

2   Second Event

3   Third Event

4   Fourth Event

5   Fifth Event

etc

12
Tactics of Play

INTRODUCTION

The objective of the game of soccer is very simple—to score more goals than the opponent. Accomplishing the objective requires stamina, enthusiasm, and knowledge of tactics. Offensive and defensive tactics of play are presented here to give coaches and parents material for the occasional BRIEF teaching point or demonstration.

Young players need lots of trial-and-error opportunities to discover how to score and prevent goals. Simple practices and small-sided scrimmages will ensure that players are having fun and learning the basics through self-discovery. Remember: let the game teach the kids!

FOUR PRINCIPLES OF OFFENSE (ATTACK)

Offensive tactics help a team maintain possession of the ball to score a goal. Visual and verbal communication are essential. The first player with the ball must make the best tactical decisions based on the abilities and positions of the other players. Penetration, support, mobility, and width are the four fundamental principles of offense. They increase the time and space in which players can dribble, pass, receive and control, and shoot the ball.

Penetration

The first attacker uses penetration to get the ball behind opponents by passing, dribbling, or shooting. At the moment the offense regains possession of a ball, players should exploit the

offensive positioning of the opponents and delay the change from offensive to defensive tactics. A long penetrating pass toward the opponent's goal can be used to put several defenders on the wrong side of the ball (Figure 12-1).

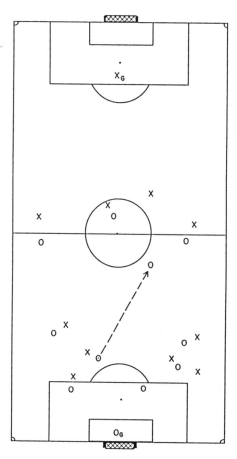

Figure 12-1. A fullback making a penetrating pass, after regaining possession of the ball. Note that with this one penetrating pass defenders are no longer in goal-side marking positions.

Support (Depth)

Offensive team members near the ball must support the player with the ball by organizing behind and in front of the first attacker. This assistance gives the player with the ball more time and space in which to play the ball. For example, a wall pass could be made backward to a supporting player to reduce pressure at the point of attack (Figure 12-2). Movements near the ball that can exploit the offensive advantage include the following:

- a **checking run** consisting of a run in one direction followed by a quick change of direction to break free of a tightly marking defender (Figure 12-3)

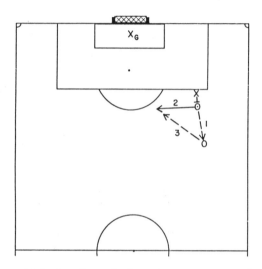

Figure 12-2. A wall pass backward to a supporting player.

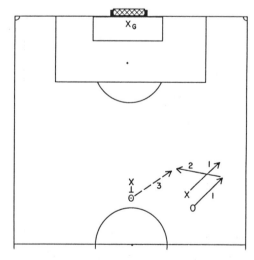

Figure 12-3. Checking run.

- an **overlapping run** involving a run from a position behind a teammate in possession of the ball to a position in advance of the ball to reduce the defensive pressure on the player with the ball (Figure 12-4)
- a **cross-over run** consisting of a dribbler and a teammate running toward each other and passing side-by-side to create confusion in the defense (Figure 12-5)

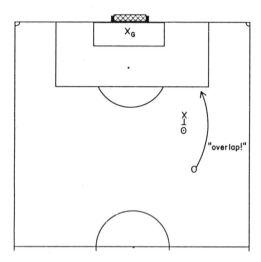

Figure 12-4. Overlapping run.

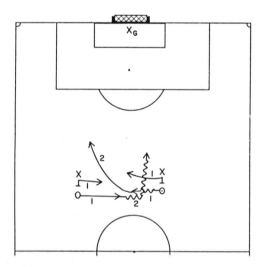

Figure 12-5. Cross-over run in which possession of the ball is exchanged by the two attackers.

Mobility

With mobility, attacking players make self-initiated runs off the ball to penetrate and unbalance the defense. Attackers who continually interchange positions force defenders to decide whether to mark these mobile players or release them to other defenders. While making these decisions, defenders may be drawn out of good defensive positions or may release attackers into open spaces where they can receive passes. Two mobility tactics are described below.

- A **blind side run** occurs when an offensive player away from the visual concentration of opponents runs to an advantageous position behind the defense (Figure 12-6)
- A **diagonal run** begins on one side of the field and progresses simultaneously toward the opponent's goal line and opposite touch line, creating confusion for the defense (Figure 12-7).

Width

The spread of offensive players from touch line to touch line determines the width of attack. Width is used to counter defensive funneling and the concentration of defenders in the danger area. Similar to the offensive principle of support, width is achieved by the positioning and movement of attacking players off the ball (Figure 12-8).

- The **dummy run** is intended to draw one or more defensive players away from a particular area of the field (Figure 12-9).

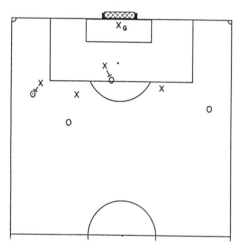

Figure 12-8. Use of width and depth in the forward "line" to counter defensive funneling and the concentration of defenders in the danger area.

Figure 12-6. Blind-side run on the side of the field opposite to where the ball is located.

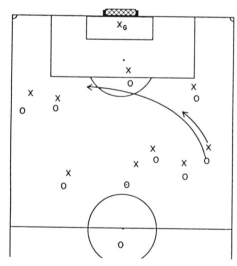

Figure 12-7. Diagonal run.

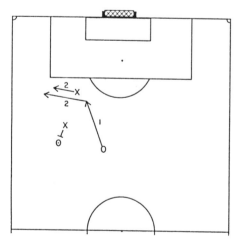

Figure 12-9. Dummy run to draw a defender out of a supporting position.

FOUR PRINCIPLES OF DEFENSE

Defensive tactics help a team regain possession of the ball and prevent opponents from scoring a goal. Visual and verbal communication are essential. The defender closest to the attacker with the ball (first defender) must make sound decisions about the angle and speed of the challenge based on the abilities and positions of the other players. Delay, depth, balance, and concentration are the four fundamental principles involved in all defensive tactics. These principles achieve their common objective by limiting the time and space in which opponents can dribble, pass, receive and control, and shoot the ball.

Delay (Pressure)

When possession of the ball is lost and an immediate chase to regain possession is unsuccessful, all team members should immediately switch from offense to defense. The primary task of the first defender (at the ball) is to mark the player with the ball and force the attackers to slow down so that the defense may organize. If the offense progresses toward the goal, the defense continues to apply pressure to restrict the offensive options. Delaying tactics used against the player with the ball include the following:

- **goal-side marking,** which requires the defender to be between the attacker and the defensive goal (Figure 12-10)

- a **recovery run** after a loss of possession in which the defender runs toward the goal to intercept the dribbler as far away from the goal as possible (Figure 12-11)
- **pressuring the ball** by facing and staying within about two yards of the attacker to force the offense to make a square or support pass or dribble (Figure 12-12)
- **jockeying,** if the goal-side defender is outnumbered, by giving ground to the player with the ball in order to mark or intercept passes to other players.
- **shepherding** to increase the predictability of the movements of the attacker with the ball (Figure 12-13)

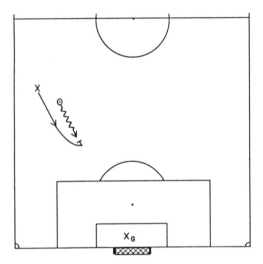

Figure 12-11. Proper and improper recovering runs. A proper recovering run to cut off the attacker relatively far from the goal.

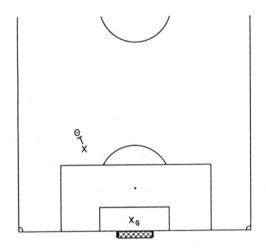

Figure 12-10. Marking a player in position of the ball. Marking from the defensive goal-side of the ball.

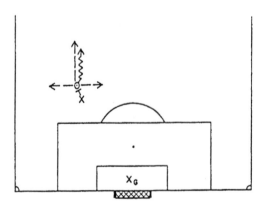

Figure 12-12. Properly delaying the attacker by pressuring the player possessing the ball to make a square pass, a support pass, or retreat dribbling.

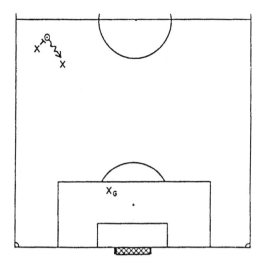

Figure 12-13. Shepherding an attacker toward a teammate.

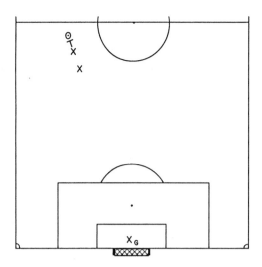

Figure 12-15. Supporting from an appropriate distance and angle.

Depth

Depth involves the use of defensive tactics to support the player marking the attacker with the ball. Defenders should organize behind the first defender to take over if the attacker with the ball gets around, or beats, the first defender. Three tactics associated with depth are:

- **covering** or closely marking players in advance of the ball (Figure 12-14)
- **supporting** a teammate who is marking the player with the ball (Figure 12-15)
- **switching** whereby a supporting defender calls "switch" and takes over marking the player with the ball, when a previous defender has been beaten (Figure 12-16)

Figure 12-16. Defensive switch with a player in a covering position.

Balance

Defenders who are not at the point of attack or positioned to support the teammate marking the attacker with the ball should focus on vital areas away from the ball that could be exploited by the attacking team. Defenders should position themselves to thwart possible penetrating attackers away from the ball. A balanced defense involves tight marking of players near the point of attack and intentional marking of vital space. Balancing tactics are described on the following page.

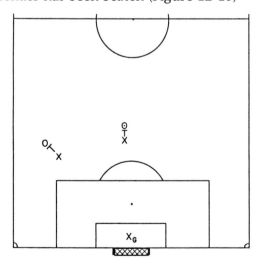

Figure 12-14. Proper position of goal-side marking and shift toward the ball.

- **Diagonal coverage** permits defenders to cover for teammates toward the ball and next to them (Figure 12-17).
- **Shifting toward the ball** by defenders who are far from the ball strengthens the defensive position (Figure 12-18).

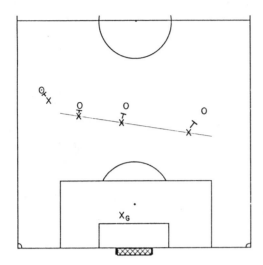

Figure 12-17. Diagonal coverage.

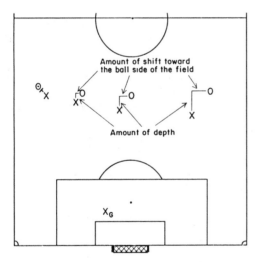

Figure 12-18. Defensive positioning based upon a combination of diagonal coverage (depth) and shifting toward the ball side of the field.

Concentration

Defensive players who are not marking the attacker with the ball should limit the offense's time and space by squeezing centrally behind the ball. Defenders who are spread out from touch line to touch line may permit attackers to play through or over the collective defending action. Three tactics associated with concentration are as follows:

- **compactness** or reducing the space between the players (closing space) by narrowing the width (touch line to touch line) and depth (goal line to goal line) of the spread (Figure 12-19)
- **overloading** by shifting to one side of the field to concentrate the team's defense (Figure 12-20)
- **funneling** by making recovering runs to the goal side of the ball (Figure 12-21).

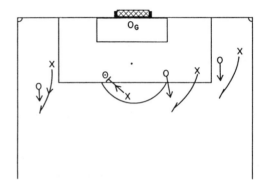

Figure 12-19. Immediately after losing possession of the ball in the offensive third of the field, the forward closest to the point of the attack marks the player with the ball while other forwards make recovering runs.

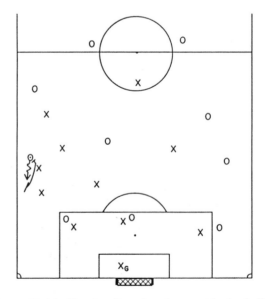

Figure 12-20. Shepherding the player with the ball toward the touch line and an overloading of the defense toward the ball-side flank.

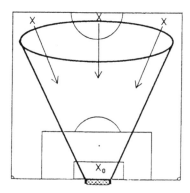

Figure 12-21. Lines of recovery associated with the defense tactic of funneling.

TEACHING TACTICS TO YOUTH PLAYERS

Coaches and parents need to overcome two challenges in teaching principles and tactics of offense and defense to youth players: limited time and the natural tendency of players to be attracted to the ball. Practice activities should move from the simple to the complex.

- Players should mimic the principle or tactic. For example, they could play handball to understand the principles of attack or defense.
- Coaches should introduce game-like exercises in which passive pressure is applied and move to exercises that involve moderate and then full pressure.
- As always, let the game teach the kids! All defensive and offensive tactics and principles can be learned in small group games, beginning with 2 v 1 and moving to 5 v 5. As the team progresses, coaches should include controlled scrimmages in practices.

Coaches can explain the principles of attack and defense by dividing the field into thirds (Figure 12-22). The safety and risk factors affect how the principles of play are applied.

- **Safety (S):** Refers to decisions made to insure security and take no unnecessary chances in offense or defense
- **Risk (R):** Refers to the degree of chance an individual or team will take in attacking or defending.

Certain elements are crucial in the defending, middle, and attacking thirds of the field.

Defending Third

- This is a no-nonsense, safety-first zone. The defense should maintain numerical superiority.
- Controlled aggression, discipline, and 1v1 defensive skills are critical.
- Pressure, cover, balance, and communication are essential.
- The goalkeeper is a key factor.

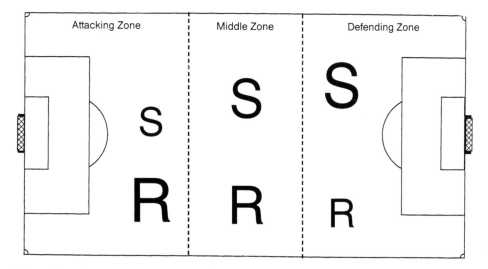

Figure 12-22. Safety (S) and Risk (R) factors affect how the principles of attack and defense are applied.

Middle Third

- In this build-up zone, ball possession is critical, and back players need time to connect and provide additional attacking options.
- The offense decides whether to possess or penetrate and must develop a rhythm.
- Attackers make connections and combine with forwards.

Attacking Third

- This is the finishing zone, so shooting is the top offensive priority.
- Players should be creatively aggressive with effective dribbling and combination plays.

METHODS OF DEFENSIVE PLAY

There are two basic methods of defensive play: zone and player-to-player defense. These two methods can also be integrated into a combination defense.

Zone Defense

In a zone defense, players are assigned to protect a particular area of the field. They are responsible for marking any player who enters their assigned zones. Adjacent zones overlap (Figure 12-23). These zones may also vary, depending on the location of the ball and the attackers. As the defensive team retreats toward its goal, the areas that its players are assigned to protect retreat with them (Figure 12-24). Similarly, if the attacking team plays the ball near a touch line, the zones shift as well (Figure 12-25). As the defense retreats, the zones should become more compact, in accordance with the fundamental defensive principle of concentration. The zone defense offers the following advantages

- Players are assigned to protect vital areas of the field.
- The zone defense is flexible.
- Defenders are more concerned with the ball than they are with following an attacker around the field.
- On small field, unprotected space is less likely.
- The zone defense is advantageous for relatively unfit players.

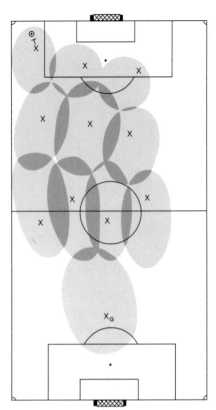

Figure 12-23. Zone responsibilities upon loss on possession in the attacking third of the field in a 4-3-3 team formation.

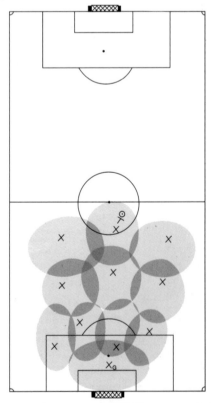

Figure 12-24. Zone responsibilities in a 4-3-3 team formation as a team retreats to its defensive half of the field.

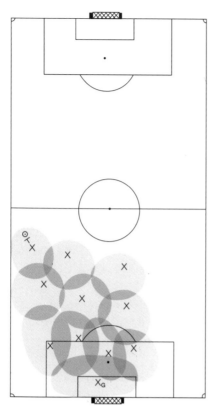

Figure 12-25. Zone responsibilities in response to a ball near the touch line in a 4-3-3 team formation.

- The zone defense is compatible with individual defense tactics of shepherding, covering, supporting, switching, diagonal coverage, shifting toward the ball, compactness, overloading, and funneling.
- It is easier to make a transition from offense to defense using a zone than it is with man-to-man.
- It is a balanced defense.
- It is easy for beginning players to learn.

Disadvantages of the zone defense are listed below:

- Any zone can be exploited by an attack that overloads a particular zone.
- When attackers move from one zone to another, defenders often have difficulty passing on responsibility to the teammate in the adjacent zone.
- Individual mistakes can be more easily hidden in a zone defense.
- Players tend to be less motivated when they play a zone defense.
- Players may be more concerned about protecting an assigned space, when no attackers are present, than in assisting teammates who need help in adjacent zones.

Player-to-Player Defense

In a strict player-to-player defense, each field player is assigned one attacker to mark. This type of marking is basic to all methods of defensive play. When a team using a player-to-player defense loses possession of the ball, its members must quickly make a transition to defense by seeking out the players they were assigned to mark. The player assigned to mark the attacker in possession of the ball must rapidly close space to prevent or impede a quick and deep penetration. The advantages of the player-to-player defense are listed below.

- An excellent attacker may be nullified by a good defender.
- An attacker may get tired trying to get free from a tenacious defender.
- Each defender has a clearly defined responsibility.
- Tight marking tends to demoralize some attackers.
- One-on-one marking permits a matching of players by ability, speed, fitness, and strength.
- It is easy to detect breakdowns.

Disadvantages of the player-to-player defense are listed below.

- Defenders can be pulled away from vital areas of the field.
- Upon loss of possession, it is more difficult for defenders to track down the players to which they are assigned than it is to retreat to assigned zones.
- It is tiring to mark one-on-one.
- Player-to-player defense requires high levels of fitness.
- If an attacker cannot be covered effectively by one defender, the attacker will continually create problems for a player-to-player defense.
- Defenders may become too concerned about the attackers they are marking and lose track of the ball's location.

SYSTEMS OF PLAY

As youth players develop, coaches will assess their strengths and weaknesses in order to select a system or formation from which the team will generally operate. For example, the 4-3-3 formation refers to the deployment of field players in this manner:

- 4 defenders
- 3 midfielders
- 3 forwards (Goalkeeper is constant)

Regardless of the system or formation, players must follow the principles of attack and defense. The system is only as strong as the players. Youth coaches should give all players opportunities to play all positions, particularly from the ages of 6 to 14. Locking a youngster into a single position during the critical stages of fun, self-discovery, and development could hinder the evolution of the total player. There will be ample opportunity for refinement and specialization later in a player's soccer career.

Coaches should take several factors into consideration when arranging players into a system of play.

- The system should fit the physical, technical, tactical, and psychological qualities of the players.
- A well-balanced team needs players who can score goals, create goals, and defend.

- Individual players will gravitate toward areas of the field that suit their "comfort zones."
- Left- or right-sided players should be positioned accordingly.
- Even the most attack-oriented team must have a balance of depth in midfield and discipline at the back to prevent constant counter attacks.
- The most defense-oriented team cannot remain on its own third or half of the field if it wants to score.

While most coaches want teams to achieve a balance and cover as much of the field as possible, the general goals are:

- numbers up in defense
- numbers up or even at midfield
- numbers down in attack

Many coaches will play out of a basic 3-3-3 to distribute the workload evenly and cover the field economically in both defense and attack. The deployment of the remaining player will be based on the needs of the team, the opposition's system, the weather, and the score and circumstances of a particular game.

13
Prevention & Treatment of Common Soccer Injuries

INTRODUCTION

Soccer involves the application of large muscular forces and physical contact at all levels of the game. Collisions between players and balls, goal posts, the ground, and other players are inevitable. Coaches and parents are responsible for doing everything reasonable to give players the chance to compete in a healthy and safe environment.

EQUIPMENT AND APPAREL

A properly equipped and attired soccer player is less likely to be injured. Essential protective equipment for all soccer players includes a ball in good condition, shin guards, well-fitting shoes, and a mouth guard. Goalkeepers need gloves, shirt, pants, helmet, and an athletic supporter with a cup or an athletic bra.

Parents should select appropriate soccer equipment and apparel for their children. If eyeglasses are essential, they should be safety glasses worn with a strap. Jewelry should never be allowed in practices or games.

At the start of the first practice, and periodically thereafter, coaches should confirm that:

- all players have essential protective equipment
- all players are properly attired
- equipment is in good repair
- equipment fits each player

The team's equipment bag should contain spare shin guards, balls, and a first aid kit. You could volunteer to solicit donated items for the equipment bag from team families, and bring the bag to all practices and games.

FACILITIES

Coaches and parents must inspect the facilities for safety hazards before permitting players to practice and play. Three categories of safety hazards are associated with facilities: field conditions, structural hazards, and environmental hazards. Safety problems that cannot be readily corrected must be promptly reported, verbally and in writing, to the responsible party. Adults should never permit children to play in unsafe conditions.

Field Conditions

Large ruts, rocks, and holes are distracting and dangerous. Playable fields can quickly deteriorate with excessive water buildup and mud from rain. Playing soccer on a wet field is not only hazardous to the participants, but may also ruin the field for subsequent play. Broken glass is another hazard that must be removed. Remove sprinklers and cover all drains.

Structural Hazards

The two structures required by the rules of play are goals and corner flags. The goals must be soundly constructed with no sharp protrusions. The corner flags must be at least 5 feet tall with non-pointed tops. Flexible posts are recommended.

Environmental Hazards

Lightning, high winds, snow, hail, temperature extremes, humidity, and rain can be extremely dangerous. Regardless of the importance of a game or practice, never run the risk of a fatality or injury from weather-related conditions. Insufficient light should be avoided with effective scheduling.

MANAGEMENT OF PRACTICES AND GAMES

Coaches and parents should take several steps to properly manage activities to minimize the rate and severity of injuries. By promoting fair play and enforcing rules, you demonstrate that skill is the determining factor in the outcome of games.

Teaching Safety

Coaches must tell players about the risks of injury associated with certain soccer movements and describe methods for avoiding injury. Safety tips should be prudently and repeatedly interjected in activities throughout the season. Before introducing various exercises into practices, coaches should ask several safety questions.

- Is the exercise appropriate for the maturation and skill levels of these players?
- Are players sufficiently conditioned?
- Are less risky exercises available to achieve the same results?

Warming Up

Coaches and parents should insist on brief warm-ups at the beginning of practices and before games. As players arrive, direct them to an area in which they can gently run in place and perform stretches under the supervision of an adult (Table 13-1). Warming up provides several benefits:

- increases the breathing rate, heart rate, and muscle temperature of each player

Table 13-1. Warm-up activities (after running slowly in place for a few minutes).

Exercises	Muscles and Joints Affected
Seated straight-leg stretch	Hamstrings, lower back, knee
Abdominal curls: bent legs, arms across chest; curl 2/3 of the way up slowly	Abdominals, lower back
Bent leg abdominal curls	Abdominals, lower back
Squat only until thigh is parallel to ground	Quadriceps
V-sit with legs spread 90° and both legs straight, or leave one leg straight and place the bottom of the foot of the bent leg up on the straight leg (next to knee)	Hamstring (straight leg); knee joint (bent leg)
Hold leg with opposite hand and extend the hip joint	Quadriceps, knee of bent leg

- reduces the risks of muscle pulls and strains
- increases the shock-absorbing capabilities of joints
- prepares the players mentally

Conditioning

Simple conditioning programs can be designed to minimize fatigue and its effects (Figure 13-1). By progressively intensifying practices throughout the season, a coach can improve the fitness levels of the players and reduce the risks of injuries.

Overtraining is also a risk for players who engage in intense, frequent practices and games, particularly near the end of the season. Telltale signs of overtraining include:

- inexplicably poor performance
- loss of enthusiasm
- depression
- higher incidence of injuries
- longer recovery times from injuries

Overtraining antidotes include time off, shorter practices, and lighter workouts. **Remember, having fun is the chief goal of most youth players.**

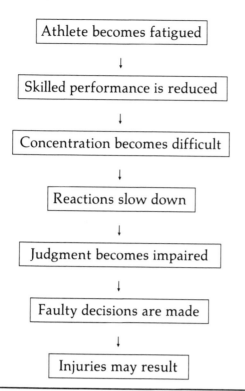

Athlete becomes fatigued

↓

Skilled performance is reduced

↓

Concentration becomes difficult

↓

Reactions slow down

↓

Judgment becomes impaired

↓

Faulty decisions are made

↓

Injuries may result

Figure 13-1. How fatigue is linked to an increased potential for injuries

Cooling Down

At the end of practices and games, coaches should lead players in a series of "winding down" activities that will allow their heart rates to lower and their muscles to relax. Repeat the warm-up activities to minimize potential stiffness, particularly after a vigorous game (Table 13-1).

EMERGENCY PROCEDURES

Despite the most diligent prevention efforts, **children do get injured** at soccer games and practices. Fortunately, these occurrences are rare and most injuries are minor. However, until the severity of the injury is assessed and corrective action taken, the coach must take charge with the support of parents and other adults. If your child is injured, you should attend to his or her needs even as you rely on the coach to resolve the overall crisis promptly and safely.

Every coach should have medical information and release forms for all players at every practice or game site at all times. THESE IN-FORMATION FORMS MAY BE LIFE-SAVING IN EMERGENCIES, AND THEY MUST

BE IN THE COACH'S POSSESSION AT ALL TIMES. ANY REPUTABLE LEAGUE WILL HAVE ITS OWN FORMS AND EMERGENCY REQUIREMENTS.

If a player is injured, the coach should take the following steps:

- Take charge with authority.
- Determine the nature of the injury.
- Start emergency procedures if necessary.
- Transfer care to a medical professional.

Take Charge

As the coach attends to the injured child, an assistant coach or another parent should take immediate charge of uninjured players by moving them to a designated area within range of the coach's voice and vision. Total silence should be enforced.

Determine the Nature of the Injury

The coach and the parent of the injured child should assess the child's condition and determine if he or she is conscious, breathing, and/or bleeding. If conscious, the player can describe the location and severity of the injury. With that information, the coach can decide if emergency measures are needed, or if the injury can be treated with routine first aid. IF THERE IS ANY UNCERTAINTY ABOUT THE SEVERITY OF A CHILD'S INJURY, IT MUST BE TREATED AS AN EMERGENCY.

Start Emergency Procedures

If the injury is serious or life-threatening, the coach should immediately order an adult to call for emergency medical services and provide information about the child's location and condition. IF CELLULAR PHONES ARE NOT AVAILABLE, COACHES MUST ALWAYS KNOW WHERE THE NEAREST PHONES ARE LOCATED AND HAVE CORRECT CHANGE AVAILABLE. Until the emergency medical personnel arrive, the coach must provide immediate treatment. The ABCs of emergency care, as advocated by the American Red Cross are:

- A=Airway (Open the airway): Check the airway to may sure it is free of any items that might impair breathing. In soccer, the mouth guard should be removed immediately. Know approved methods for opening the airway by thrusting the injured child's jaw or lifting the chin.
- B=Breathing (Restore breathing): Check to see if the player's chest is moving up and down or if exhaled air can be felt at the mouth or nostrils. If the child is not breathing, start artificial respiration according to certified instructions.
- C=Circulation (Restore circulation): If the child's heart has stopped beating, circulation should be restored via cardiopulmonary resuscitation (CPR).

If the player is bleeding profusely, the coach or parent must still follow the ABCs, because stopping the bleeding will serve no benefit if the injured player cannot breathe. Extensive bleeding should be controlled by applying direct pressure over the wound with a sterile pad, towel, shirt, or hand. A tourniquet is not appropriate unless its use is the only way to save a life.

COACHES MUST BE FAMILIAR WITH LIFE-SAVING PROCEDURES TAUGHT BY THE RED CROSS AND THROUGH MANY HOSPITALS AND SHOULD BE CERTIFIED TO ADMINISTER CPR AND FIRST AID. It is beyond the scope of this book to provide this information, but coaches are emphatically directed to obtain it. Responsible parents should confirm that youth coaches are prepared to handle life-threatening emergencies.

BACK OR NECK INJURIES

Any blow or fall that affects a child's back or neck and causes the player to become immobile or unconscious must be treated with extreme caution. Other symptoms include: pain and tenderness over the spine, numbness, weakness or heaviness in the limbs, or tingling feeling in extremities.

- The coach and parent should make sure the player is breathing, insist that he or she remain completely still, and call for medical assistance. The player may return to action only with the written permission of a physician.

HEAD INJURIES

Any injury that causes a player to lose consciousness or affects the player's ability to respond coherently to known facts (name, date, team name) may signal severe damage to the brain or spinal cord. Other symptoms include: dizziness, pupils that are unequal in size and/or non-responsive to light, disorientation, unsteady movement of eyeballs when following movement, pain or tenderness over spine, numbness, weakness or heaviness in limbs, or tingling feelings in extremities. Cuts or bruises around the head may be present.

- A conscious player should be moved to a quiet place and observed closely until medical professionals or parents arrive and thereafter for at least 24 hours.
- An unconscious player should not be moved, but if necessary, the airway should be cleared without moving the neck. Immediate medical attention is essential. With any head injury, the player may return to soccer only with the written permission of a physician.

FRACTURES

A crack or complete break in a bone is a fracture. With a simple fracture, a player's bone is broken or cracked, but the skin is not. With an open fracture, the broken bone has punctured the skin. Other symptoms include: pain at the fracture site, tenderness, swelling, deformity or unnatural position, and loss of function.

- The coach and parents should stabilize the injured bone with splints, slings, or bandages, but should not attempt to straighten the injured part while immobilizing it. If the skin is broken, keep the open wound as clean as possible by covering it with cloth or sterile gauze. Check for shock and treat if necessary until medical attention arrives, or until the player can be taken to an emergency room or physician. The player can return to action only with the written permission of a physician.

HEAT STROKE

This life-threatening heat disorder is very rare but requires urgent treatment. Its symptoms include: extremely high body temperature; hot, red, and dry skin; rapid and strong pulse; confusion; fainting; and convulsions.

- Call for emergency medical assistance and cool the body at once by cold sponging, immersion, and cold packs. The player can return to action only with the written permission of a physician.

SHOCK

This condition is the body's adverse reaction to physical or psychological trauma. Symptoms include: pallor, cold and clammy skin, dizziness, nausea, and faintness.

- Send for emergency help, and have the athlete lie down and elevate the feet, unless there is a head injury. Control the player's temperature and loosen tight-fitting clothing. Control any pain or bleeding. The player can return to action only with the written permission of a physician.

Transfer Care to a Medical Professional

If the parents of the injured child are not present when emergency technicians arrive, the coach must provide the child's medical information and release forms to the medical professionals. The coach must also direct another adult to contact the injured child's parents. It may be necessary for the coach to accompany the child in an ambulance or other emergency vehicle in the absence of the parents.

FIRST AID PROCEDURES

If soccer injuries are not life-threatening, parents and coaches can work together to provide treatment. Common medical conditions that may occur in soccer are described below. This information includes: a definition, common symptoms, immediate-on-field treatment, and guidelines for returning a player to action.

ABRASION

A superficial skin wound caused by scraping. Symptoms include: minor bleeding, redness, and a burning sensation.

- Cleanse the area with soap and water or antibacterial wipes.
- Control the bleeding.
- Cover the area with a sterile dressing.
- Monitor for several days for signs of infection.
- Return the child to action after providing immediate care.

BLISTERS

Localized collection of fluid in the outer portion of the skin. Symptoms include: redness, inflammation, oozing of fluid, and discomfort.

- Put disinfectant on the area.
- Cut a hole in a stack of gauze pads to create a donut to surround the blister.
- Cover the area with a bandage.
- Alter the cause of the problem (ill-fitting shoes, socks, etc.)
- Return to action immediately, unless pain is severe.

CONTUSION (BRUISE)

An injury in which the skin is not broken. Symptoms include: tenderness around the injury, swelling, and localized pain.

- Apply the R.I.C.E. (Rest-Ice-Compression-Elevation) formula, and suggest that the player do the same for three days.
- Restrict activity.
- Pad the bruise when the player returns.
- Return to action when there is no pain whatsoever and full range of motion is restored.

CRAMPS

Involuntary and forceful contraction or spasm of a muscle. Symptoms include: localized pain in the contracting muscle.

- Help the player slowly stretch the muscle.
- Gently massage the muscle.

- Return to action when pain is gone and full range of motion reappears.

DENTAL INJURY

Any injury to mouth or teeth. Symptoms include: pain, bleeding, and partial or total loss of tooth.

- Clear the airway if necessary, and make sure excess blood does not impair breathing.
- Stop the bleeding with direct pressure.
- Retrieve and save any teeth that were knocked free and store in a moist, sterile cloth. Do not rub or clean any tooth that has been knocked out.
- Get player to a hospital or dentist.
- Return to action when pain is gone and with permission of dentist or physician.

DISLOCATION

Loss of the normal anatomical alignment of a joint. Symptoms include: complaints of a joint slipping in and out (subluxation), a joint that is out of line, or pain at the joint.

- For a mild dislocation, treat as a sprain and apply the R.I.C.E. treatment, and seek medical attention.
- For a severe dislocation, immobilize the injured joint before moving and seek immediate medical attention.
- Return to action only with written permission of a physician.

EYE INJURY-BRUISE

A direct blow to the eye and the region surrounding the eye by a blunt object. Symptoms include: pain, redness, and watery eye.

- Tell the player to lie down and close eyes.
- Place a clean, folded cloth, soaked in cold water, gently over the eye.
- Seek medical attention if the injury looks severe.
- Return to action when the symptoms clear for a minor injury, only with permission of a physician for a severe injury.

EYE INJURY-FOREIGN OBJECT

The lodging of an object between the eyelid and the eyeball. Symptoms include: pain, redness, watery eye, and inability to keep eye open.

- Do not allow player to rub the eye.
- Allow tears to form to help flush the object out.
- Carefully try to remove a loose object with a sterile cotton swab.
- If the object is imbedded, have the player close both eyes, loosely cover both eyes with a sterile dressing, and seek immediate medical attention.
- Return to action only with the written permission of a physician.

FAINTING

Dizziness and loss of consciousness that may be caused by injury, exhaustion, heat illness, emotional stress, or lack of oxygen. Symptoms include: a spinning sensation, cold and clammy skin, pallor, seeing spots, and a weak, rapid pulse.

- Have the player lie down and elevate the feet, or have the player sit with the head between the knees.
- Observe the player closely for the remainder of the game or practice.
- Return to action only with written permission of a physician.

HEAT EXHAUSTION

A heat disorder that may lead to heat stroke. Symptoms include: fatigue, profuse sweating, chills, throbbing pressure in the head, nausea, normal body temperature, pale and clammy skin, and muscle cramps.

- Remove the player from the heat and sun.
- Provide plenty of water
- Rest the player on his back with feet elevated about twelve inches.
- Loosen or remove the player's clothing.
- Fan the athlete.
- Drape wet towels over the athlete.
- Return to action the next day if symptoms are no longer present.

LACERATIONS

Tears or cuts in the skin. Symptoms include: bleeding and swelling.

- Elevate the area and apply direct pressure with gauze to stop bleeding.
- Clean the wound with disinfectant.
- Apply the R.I.C.E. formula.
- If stitches are needed, obtain within 6 hours.
- Return to action as soon as pain is gone, if wound can be protected from further injury.

LOSS OF WIND

A forceful blow to the mid-abdomen region that causes an inability to breathe. Symptoms include: rapid, shallow breathing and gasping for breath.

- Check player to see if other injuries exist.
- Have player lay down with the face up.
- Calm player down to encourage slower breathing.
- Return to action after five minutes of rest if breathing has returned to normal.

NOSE BLEED

Bleeding from the nose. Other symptoms include: swelling, pain, and deformity of nose.

- Calm the athlete, and place him or her in a sitting position.
- Pinch the nostrils together while the athlete breathes through the mouth.
- If bleeding cannot be controlled, seek medical assistance.
- Return to action when bleeding has stopped for several minutes and nose can be packed with gauze unless fracture is a possibility, in which case, only with the written permission of a physician.

PUNCTURE WOUND

Any hole made by the piercing of a pointed instrument. Symptoms include: breakage of skin, minor or no bleeding, and tenderness around the wound.

- Control bleeding.
- Cleanse the area with soap and water or anti-bacterial wipes.
- Cover the area with a sterile dressing.
- Tell parents to consult physician about a tetanus shot and monitor for several days for infection.
- Return to action with permission from physician.

SPRAIN

A stretching or partial or complete tear of the ligaments surrounding a joint. Symptoms include: pain at the joint, pain aggravated by movement, tenderness and swelling, and looseness at the joint.

- Immobilize at the time of the injury if pain is severe; may use corner flag post as a splint.
- Apply R.I.C.E. and tell parents to take player to physician.
- Return to action when pain and swelling are gone, full range of motion is reestablished, strength and stability are near normal, and when there is no favoring of the injury.

STRAIN

A stretching or tearing of the muscle or tendons that attach the muscle to the bone. Symptoms include: localized pain brought on by movement of the muscle in question and unequal strength between limbs.

- Apply R.I.C.E. and tell parents to use contrast treatments.
- Return to action when the player can stretch the injured segment as far as the non-injured segment, when strength in both segments is equal, and when player does not favor the injured part (this can take from one day to two weeks).

14
Glossary of Soccer Terms

Advantage (Advantage Clause) Refers to part of Law V (Referees) of the Laws of the Game. It gives the referee the right to refrain from penalizing in cases where calling a penalty would give an advantage to the offending team (e.g., A defender attempting to trip an attacking player, who is dribbling the ball into position to take a shot on goal, should not be called for the foul unless the attacker has been prevented from advancing the ball.).

Air Ball Any ball that is not in contact with the ground.

Arc (see **Penalty Arc**)

Attack (Attacking Team) The team in possession of the ball.

Attacker A player on the team in possession of the ball can be called an attacker. However, "attacker" usually refers to players in scoring positions.

Back A general name given to a fullback and other field players whose roles are primarily defensive.

Back Door The most common use of this term refers to the space behind the defense on weak side of the field.

Back-Heel A pass in which the heel is used to contact the ball centrally but not always backwards.

Ball-Side Pertains to the side of the field (in a lengthwise division of the field) where the ball is located (e.g., A ball-side back is a fullback located on the same side of field as the ball.).

Banana (Banana Kick) A ball kicked that curves laterally (see **Bending the Ball**).

Beat The act of getting to the ball before an opponent, or when in possession of the ball, outmaneuvering an opponent to get past him/her.

Bending the Ball Refers to the technique of kicking the ball with an off-center (right or left) and oblique strike by the foot, so that the ball has lateral spin, resulting in a curved path (see **Banana**).

Bending Run A curved run made by an offensive player to get into position to receive a pass or to possibly draw defenders.

Bicycle Kick A kick that is made with the body off the ground and leaning backwards. Initially, the non-kicking leg is swung forward and upward and the kicking leg lags behind. The legs then rapidly switch positions (see **Scissors Kick**) and the kicking foot contacts the ball to drive it back and over the head of the kicker.

Blind-Side Run A run made by an offensive player in an area of the field away from the visual concentration of opponents (i.e., opposite to the ball-side of the field).

Block Tackle The block tackle refers to the use of the inside of the foot to "block" the movement of the ball at the same time as the opponent attempts to kick or dribble it forward.

Boots Another name for soccer shoes or cleats.

Breakaway This situation occurs when the player with the ball is beyond all the defending field players and has an unchallenged path, except for possibly the goalkeeper, to the goal.

Bunch (Bunching) A close gathering of two or more players from the same team (offense or defense).

Carry (Carrying) A player who maintains the dribble carries the ball. Coaches will often call "carry" if they want their player to continue to dribble the ball.

Catenaccio The Italian word for "bolt." Catenaccio described the man-to-man defensive system of marking used by the Italians in the 1950s. In this system, one player (the Libero or free back) played behind the other field players to provide defensive support.

Caution   An official action taken by the referee against any player who (a) enters or leaves the field of play without permission, (b) persistently infringes upon the Laws of the Game, (c) shows by word or action dissent toward any decision given by the referee, or (d) is guilty of unsportsmanlike behavior. The referee signifies a caution by holding up a yellow card to the player.

Center (Centering Pass)   A long pass that is made from the side of the field to the area in front of the goal (see **Cross**).

Center Back   Refers to the center fullback.

Center Circle   A circle at the center of the field drawn with a 10-yard radius from the center mark. The center circle is used for kickoffs to start either half of play and to restart play after a goal is scored.

Center Forward   This player is a principal attacker who is positioned at the center of the forward line.

Center Line   (see **Halfway Line**)

Center Mark   This mark is at the center of the halfway line. It is used for kickoffs.

Change of Field (Change Fields)   Refers to a pass from one side of the field to the other (see **Cross**).

Charge (Charging)   The term "charge" describes allowed intentional contact between players. This allowed contact (a) must be shoulder to shoulder with arms (especially elbows) close to the body, (b) is permitted only while the ball is near enough to play, (c) must be intended to gain possession of the ball and not to knock down or injure an opponent, and (d) is permitted when at least one foot of each player is in contact with the ground. If the charge is not performed in this manner, it may result in a foul.

Checking Run   An offensive maneuver consisting of a run in one direction followed by a quick change of direction. A checking run is used to free an offensive player from a tightly marking defender.

Chip   The act of lofting a ball from the ground into the air by kicking it below its center. This technique can be used to pass (Chip Pass) or shoot (Chip Shot) the ball.

Clear (Clearance)   This occurs when defending players project the ball far away from their own goal to decrease their opponent's immediate chances of scoring. Clears can be made by field players and goalkeepers.

Close Space   Describes a condition in which one or more defenders are positioned between a player with the ball and another player on attack. This defensive arrangement is desirable because an attempted pass between these two attackers is likely to be intercepted.

Club Linesman (Club Linesperson)   A person appointed by the referee whose only role is to indicate when a ball has gone out of play.

Corner Area   A quarter of a circle, at each of the four corners of the field. The corner area is marked on the field with a one-yard radius from the corner flag.

Corner Flag   A flag on the non-pointed top of a post, not less than five feet in height. Corner flags are used to designate each of the four corners of the field of play.

Contain   Refers to any defensive technique or tactic that is used to restrict an opponent to a certain area of the field.

Counter (Counterattack)   An attack that is begun immediately after gaining possession of the ball.

Cover   The term cover is used in three different ways in soccer. The term is generally used to describe close marking or guarding of an offensive player who does not have possession of the ball. It is also used to describe the action of a free defender who is ready to take over for a teammate guarding the player with the ball. Finally, it also refers to close marking of offensive players in advance of the ball.

Cross (Crossing Ball)   A pass, usually in the air, that is kicked from one side of the field to the other (see **Change of Field**) or from one side of the field to the area in front of the goal (see **Center**).

Cross Bar   The part of the goal that is parallel to the ground and directly over the goal line. It provides for a 24-foot-wide opening to the goal.

Cross-Over Run (Take-Over Run)   When a dribbler and teammate run toward each other and they pass by side-by-side, they have completed a cross-over run. At the point their paths cross, possession of the ball may be exchanged (take-over).

Curving the Ball   (see **Bending the Ball**)

Cushioning the Ball   Refers to the action of a relaxed body part that a player uses to absorb and yield to the impact force of a soccer ball to decrease its pace when attempting to receive and control the ball.

Cutting Down the Angle (see **Narrowing the Angle**)

Danger Area (Danger Zone) Generally refers to the space in front of the goal where an offensive player in possession of the ball is a threat to score.

Dangerous Play Any activity that may result in an injury to an opponent, teammate, or player performing the action may be interpreted by the referee as dangerous play. Dangerous play is a non-penal foul, which results in an indirect free kick.

Dead Ball A ball that is not in play. A dead ball occurs when a ball passes out of the field of play, during a temporary suspension of play caused by an infraction, or when the game is otherwise stopped by the referee.

Decreasing the Angle (see **Narrowing the Angle**)

Defender Any player on the team that is not in possession of the ball may be called a defender.

Defense Refers to all techniques and tactics that are used to regain possession of the ball and to prevent the opposing team from scoring.

Deflecting (Parrying) This term describes the action taken by a goalkeeper in which one or two open hands are used to redirect a shot away from the goal.

Delay A fundamental principle of defense in which players attempt to impede the progress of the offensive team to gain time to incorporate more players in defense and to employ other defensive tactics.

Depth The positioning of players on the field from goal line to goal line, to provide mutual tactical assistance in either offensive or defensive play is called depth.

Diagonal Run A run on offense that begins near one touch line and progresses simultaneously toward the opponent's goal line and opposite touch line.

Diagonal System (see **Three-Man System**)

Direct Free Kick A place kick that is awarded to a team as a result of a penal foul being committed against them. The kick is taken from the point of the infraction and a goal may be scored directly from the kick.

Distribution Refers to the various individual techniques used by a player to pass the ball to teammates. It is more frequently used to describe this activity when performed by a goalkeeper.

Down Field Away from where the ball is located and toward the opposite goal.

Down the Line Describes a ball passed near a touch line and toward the opponent's goal.

Dribble (Dribbling) The act of maneuvering the ball on the ground while maintaining control of it by a series of touches with different parts of the feet.

Drive (Drive the Ball) A powerful kick, usually associated with a ball projected low to the ground, is called a drive.

Drop Ball The method used by a referee to start play after it has been stopped for an injury, a foreign object on the field, or other circumstances when no laws of the game have been violated. The ball is dropped by the referee. The ball is back into play after it strikes the ground.

Drop Kick A distribution technique used by the goalkeeper. It is performed by dropping the ball from the hands to the ground and then immediately kicking it as a half volley.

Dual System (see **Two-Man System**)

Dummy Run An offensive run intended to draw one or more defenders away from a particular area of the field without the ball.

Ejection An official action taken by the referee against any player who (a) is guilty of violent conduct or serious foul play, (b) uses foul or abusive language, and (c) persists in misconduct after having received a caution. The referee signifies an ejection by holding up a red card to the player. The team whose player is ejected completes the game short one player on the field.

Far Post The goal post farthest away from the player with the ball.

Feint Action taken by a player that is intended to deceive an opponent. This action may involve movements of body parts and/or movements of the ball.

Field Player Any soccer player other than a goalkeeper.

FIFA An acronym for Federation Internationale de Football Association, which is the international governing body of soccer.

Finish (Finishing) Refers to a shot on goal to complete an attack.

First Defender Player marking the attacker with the ball.

First Time Describes the method of kicking an approaching ball that involves passing or shooting it without first attempting to receive and control the ball.

Flank Refers to the area of the field within approximately 15 feet of either touch line.

Football Term used internationally for the game North Americans call soccer.

Foot Plant (see **Planted Foot**)

Formation The general organization of players to prescribed positions on the field. It is noted by a numerical grouping of the ten field players proceeding from those closest to the goalkeeper to those closest to the opponent's goal (e.g., A 4-3-3 is a formation that uses 4 fullbacks, 3 halfbacks, and 3 forwards, as well as a goalkeeper.).

Forward Refers to any of the players on the front line of the team's formation.

Foul There are two types of fouls—the five non-penal fouls and the nine penal fouls (see **Non-Penal Foul** and **Penal Foul**).

Free Back A defender positioned behind the fullbacks, who is free to support and cover for whichever fullback needs help (see **Catenaccio**, **Libero**, and **Sweeper**).

Free Kick A place kick that is awarded to a team that has been fouled. There are two types of free kicks—direct and indirect (see **Direct Free Kick** and **Indirect Free Kick**).

Fullback A player in the team's last line of defense located immediately in front of the goalkeeper.

Funnel (Funneling) Refers to the defensive retreat of players toward their own goal, upon losing possession of the ball, from positions on the flanks to central positions. Funneling results in a concentration of defenders in front of their own goal. Funneling limits the attacking space available to opponents in the danger area.

Give and Go (see **Wall Pass**)

Goal Refers to the target at each end of the field of play (8 feet high by 8 yards wide) for 12 years and older, also a score that is made by projecting the ball into this target.

Goal Area A rectangular area (six yards by 20 yards) that is marked on each end of the field of play. One of the 20 yard sides of each of the rectangles is centered on each of the goal lines. The goal area is primarily used to designate the location to take goal kicks.

Goalkeeper (Goalie, Keeper) This player is usually the last line of defense. With few exceptions, the goalkeeper is controlled by the same rules as the field players. The primary difference is that the goalkeepers are permitted to use their hands on the ball in their own penalty area.

Goal Kick A free kick taken from the goal area. It is a kick that is awarded to the defending team when the ball is played over their goal line by the attacking team. The ball is not back into play from a goal kick until it passes out of the penalty area and onto the field.

Goal Line The two goal lines are the boundary lines located at the ends of the field. They extend from touch line to touch line and pass directly beneath the cross bars of each goal.

Goal Mouth The area immediately in front of the goal.

Goal Post The vertical or upright posts that are perpendicular to the goal line. They support the horizontal cross bar at a height of eight feet above the ground.

Goal-Side Refers to a position between the ball and the goal being defended (e.g., goal-side marking).

Grid A series of square or rectangular spaces that are marked on the field. Exercises and small-sided games are organized by coaches in these restricted spaces to teach their players techniques and tactics.

Ground Ball Any ball that is rolling or bouncing on the field.

Halfback (see **Midfielder**)

Halftime The period between the two halves of the game. The rules governing the game designate its length.

Half Volley An air ball that is kicked or received immediately after it strikes the ground.

Half Way Line This line divides the field into two equal halves. It runs widthwise and connects the two touch lines.

Hand Ball (Hands) A penal foul that occurs when field players intentionally play the ball with their hands or arms. Goalkeepers are bound by this rule except when playing a ball within their own penalty area. Note that in some leagues females are permitted to use their arms when making a chest trap.

Head (Heading, Header) Refers to any of several individual techniques used by older players in which the head is used to pass, shoot, or receive a ball. Contact is usually made with the forehead.

Heel Pass (see **Back-Heel**)

Hitch Kick (see **Bicycle Kick** and **Scissors Kick**)

Hold (Holding) A penal foul that occurs when a player grasps an opponent with any part of a hand or arm.

Improvise (Improvisation) Refers to the ability of an attacking player to be creative and adapt to situations as they occur.

Indirect Free Kick A place kick that is awarded to a team as a result of an infraction committed against them. A goal cannot be scored directly from an indirect free kick; after the kick, the ball must make contact with another player from either team before a goal may be scored. An indirect free kick is taken from the point of the infraction, unless it is committed in an opponent's goal area. In that circumstance, the kick may be taken from any point within the half of the goal area (right or left) in which the infraction occurred.

Inside Forward Refers to a player on the forward line who is neither a wing nor a center forward.

Instep Refers to the lace portion of the shoes. It is used in various individual techniques to kick and receive a ball.

Inswinger A cross that curves toward the goal. This term is most often associated with long corner kicks.

Jockey (Jockeying) Refers to a delay tactic used by a defensive player. In jockeying, a defender may repeatedly feint making a tackle and giving ground to disrupt advances of the dribbler and provide teammates with time to recover.

Juggle (Juggling) An individual training technique that is used to develop control of the ball. Juggling consists of keeping the ball in the air by repeatedly hitting it with various parts of the body except the hands and arms.

Kickoff An indirect free kick, taken from the center of the field, that is used to start play at the beginning of each half and after each goal.

Laws of the Game These are the 17 rules, according to FIFA, that govern the play of the game of soccer.

Lead Pass A pass that is kicked to a point in front of a teammate. It is usually intended to permit the teammate to continue to run and receive the ball without altering stride.

Legal Charge (see **Charge**).

Libero The Italian word for free back (see **Catenaccio, Free Back,** and **Sweeper**).

Linesmen (Linespersons) These are two officials whose duties are to indicate (a) when the ball is out of play; (b) which side is entitled to a corner kick, goal kick, or throw-in; and (c) when a substitution is desired. In general they are responsible for assisting the referee.

Linkman (see **Midfielder**).

Lob A ball that is kicked high into the air over the heads of opponents.

Lofted Ball A ball that is kicked high into the air by using either a chip, a half volley, or a volley.

Long Corner (Long Corner Kick) A corner kick in which a centering pass is made to put the ball back into play.

Looking Off the Ball (see **Off the Ball**)

"Man On" A call made by a coach or player to warn a team member in possession of the ball or about to receive the ball that a defender will be marking.

Man-to-Man (Person-to-Person) A style of defense in which one or more players are assigned to guard specific attackers.

Mark Another term for guard.

Match A synonym for an official soccer game.

Midfield A widthwise portion of the field that encompasses about the middle third of the field.

Midfielder (Midfield Player) A player who has primary offensive and defensive responsibilities in the middle third of the field. Midfielders are also called linkmen and halfbacks because they serve as a connection between the forwards and fullbacks.

Mobility A basic offensive concept associated with movement of attackers, who are not in possession of the ball, to use existing space and create new space into which passes and other runs can be made.

Narrowing the Angle Refers to the action taken by a goalkeeper who quickly advances, under control, along an imaginary line connecting the center of the goal line and the ball. (This action reduces the open angle that an attacker has to shoot on goal.)

Near Post The goal post closest to the player with the ball.

Neutral Linesman (Neutral Linesperson) (see **Club Linesman**).

Non-Penal Foul Fouls that are less serious than penal fouls. They result in an indirect free kick to be taken by the fouled team from the point of the infraction.

Nutmeg A slang term used to describe a situation in which an attacker advances the ball by passing it between the defender's legs.

Obstruction A deliberate movement by a player intended to impede an opponent. Obstruction is penalized by awarding the obstructed player's team an indirect free kick. Note that if the obstruction occurs within playing distance of the ball, a foul is not committed.

Off the Ball Refers to a location on the field that is not in the vicinity of the ball. (e.g., An attacking player may make a run off the ball. A dribbler may look off the ball.)

Offside An illegal offensive position of players in advance of the ball. It is the most complex law within the game. Consult Law XI of the Laws of the Game for the details of this infraction.

Offside Position A player must be illegally positioned in advance of the ball (offside position) in order to be offside. However, an offside infraction should not be called unless a player is seeking to gain an advantage from this positioning.

Offside Trap A defensive maneuver designed to put attacking players offside. This usually involves fullbacks quickly moving away from their own goal to create a situation in which attackers are positioned illegally in advance of the ball.

"On" An abbreviation for "man on" (see **"Man On"**).

One time (See **One Touch**).

One Touch Describes the method of passing or shooting an approaching ball without first attempting to receive and control it; in other words, the ball is kicked on the first touch.

Open Space Describes a condition in which no defenders are positioned between the player with the ball and a teammate. This offensive arrangement is desirable because a pass can freely be made without the likelihood of an interception.

Outside Forward Refers to a player on either end of the forward line who is positioned nearest the touch line (see **Outside Left, Outside Right,** and **Wing**).

Outside Fullback Refers to a player on either end of the fullback line who is positioned nearest the touch line.

Outside Left The player on the left end of the forward line. This player is also called the left wing.

Outside Right The player on the right end of the forward line. This player is also called the right wing.

Outswinger A cross that curves away from the goal. This term is most often associated with corner kicks.

Overlap (Overlapping Run) Occurs when an offensive player runs from a position behind a teammate in possession of the ball to a position in advance of the ball. An overlapping run decreases pressure at the point of attack by either drawing the defender away from the player with the ball or providing an opportunity for the player with the ball to make a pass to the teammate running into open space.

Own Goal A score resulting from a ball that is inadvertently played by a defender into his/her own goal.

Passive Pressure Inactive opposition to a player in possession of the ball. Passive pressure can be used as a lead-up technique in teaching various individual offensive techniques or it can be used in the game as a delay tactic to slow the advance of an attacking team.

Penal Fouls These are serious fouls. They result in a direct free kick to be taken by the fouled team from the point of the infraction. Note that if a penal foul is committed by a player in his/her own penalty area, a penalty kick is awarded to the fouled team.

Penalty Arc The portion of the circumference of a circle, with a 10-yard radius and center at the penalty kick mark, that extends outside the penalty area. It is used as a restraining line for players during the taking of a penalty kick.

Penalty Area A rectangular area (18 yards by 44 yards) that is marked on each end of the field of play. One of the 44 yard sides of each of the rectangles is centered on each of the goal lines. The area is used to (a) determine if a penalty kick should be awarded to a team sustaining a penal foul, (b) restrict players during the taking of a penalty kick, and (c) limit the area in which goalkeepers can use their hands.

Penalty Kick A direct free kick taken from the penalty kick mark. It is awarded as the result of a penal foul committed by a team in their own penalty area. At the time the penalty kick is taken, the goalkeeper must be standing with both feet stationary on the goal line. All other players except for the kicker must be outside the penalty area and at least 10 yards from the ball (outside the penalty arc).

Penalty Kick Mark (Penalty Kick Spot, Penalty Kick Line) A mark on the field, 12 yards from the center of the goal line, that is used as a location from which penalty kicks are taken.

Penetrating Pass (see **Through Pass**)

Penetration Refers to the action of an attacking team that quickly advances the ball through the defense and creates scoring opportunities.

Pitch A British name for a soccer field.

Place Kick Refers to "kickoff" start of game, start of or second half or after a goal is scored.

Planted Foot Usually refers to the support foot (non-kicking foot) that is set firmly on the ground when making a kick. The term also refers to a foot that provides support to the body when a player performs other movements such as pivots, jumps, and tackles.

Point of Attack The location of the ball when it is in the possession of a player.

Position (Positioning) A player's assigned location and/or responsibility with a team's general organization on the field (e.g., goalkeeper, center halfback, right wing (see **Formation**).

Preferred Foot The dominant or favorite foot of a player.

Pressure (Pressuring, Pressurize) A delay tactic associated with the restriction of the attackers' time and space.

Professional Foul   A foul that is intentionally committed to take away an opponent's advantage.

Punch (Punching)   Describes the action taken by a goalkeeper in which one or both fists are used to knock a shot away from the goal.

Punt   An individual distribution technique that is used by goalkeepers to clear the ball away from their goal. In punting, the ball is released from the hands and then kicked with the instep.

Push (Pushing)   A penal foul that is committed when players use their hands to move an opponent or when they rest their hands on an opponent.

Push Pass   Another term for an inside of the foot kick in which the ball is passed on the ground over a short distance.

Quick Kick   The rapid taking of any free kick without waiting for defenders to be positioned 10 or more yards from the ball.

Read (Reading the Game, Reading the Play)   Refers to the ability of a player to analyze and interpret a game situation, anticipate the outcome, and quickly and appropriately respond.

Recovery Run (Recovering Run)   A defensive run to get to a goal side marking position.

Referee   The appointed official in charge of the game. The referee is empowered by the Laws of the Game.

Restart   Describes all methods used to recommence play after it has been stopped. The following is a listing of all restarts: drop ball, throw-in, goal kick, direct free kick, indirect free kick, kick off, corner kick, and penalty kick.

Running Off the Ball   (see **Off the Ball**)

Save   Refers to the various individual techniques associated with catching, punching, and deflecting a ball that are used by the goalkeeper to prevent a goal.

Scissors Kick   Refers to any kick performed by a player while off the ground in which the non-kicking foot is swung forward and then back, exchanging positions with the kicking foot. Contact with the ball is made on the forward swing of the kicking foot (see **Bicycle Kick**).

Score   Refers to a goal (point) awarded when the entire ball passes over the goal line, between the goal posts, and under the cross bar.

Screen   Refers to a player or group of players positioning themselves so their bodies obstruct their opponent's view of the ball. This term is sometimes synonymously used for shielding (see **Shield**).

Second Defender   Any defensive player engaged in supporting, or to assist a teammate marking the player with the ball.

Set Play (Set Piece)   Refers to a predetermined tactic that is usually employed in restart situations.

Shepherd (Shepherding)   A defensive tactic that involves channeling and jockeying of opponents so they move or pass the ball into locations on the field that are not as likely to result in scoring opportunities.

Shield (Shielding)   Refers to the positioning of a player in possession of the ball, between an opponent and the ball. Players shield the ball with their bodies to prevent opponents from gaining possession of the ball. Shielding may or may not be legal, depending on whether or not an opponent is being obstructed (see **Obstruction**).

Short Corner (Short Corner Kick)   A corner kick in which a short pass is used to put the ball back into play.

Shot   A kick, head, or any intended deflection of the ball toward a goal by a player attempting to score a goal.

Shoulder Charge   (see **Charge**)

Side Line   (see **Touch Line**)

Side Volley   A variation of an instep volley in which an air ball, located to the side of the body, is kicked. When making a side volley, the player's trunk leans away from the ball and approaches a horizontal orientation.

Skills   Individual techniques such as receiving and controlling the ball with the chest, kicking the ball with the outside of the foot, and marking an opponent in possession of the ball become skills when they are used under game conditions.

Slide Tackle (Sliding Tackle)   Refers to any attempt to dispossess an opponent of the ball in which the defensive player slides to the ground in making the tackle (see **Tackle**).

Small-Sided Games   Refers to play during practices or modified match competition in which fewer than 11 players per team are employed.

Space   (see **Close Space** and **Open Space**).

Square Pass   Refers to (a) a pass that is laterally made with respect to the field, or (b) a pass by a player to his/her side.

Stopper   A defender who is centrally located in front of the fullbacks.

Strategy   (see **Tactics**).

Striker   Generally refers to any player in a forward position who has relatively frequent opportunities to shoot on goal. This term, however, is more frequently used to describe an inside or center forward.

Strong Foot The preferred or dominant foot of a player.

Style of Play Refers to the nature of play demonstrated by an individual or a team. The following terms are some examples of descriptors of style: short passing, long passing, direct play, aggressive play, finesse, counterattacking, defensive, and offensive.

Substitute (Substitution) This is a player who replaces a teammate on the field. Substitutions must be made in accordance with the rules of competition under which the game is being played. In most youth games, an unlimited number of substitutions may be made. These usually occur at the start of any period (e.g., halftime, overtime); after a goal is scored; before a goal kick; and before a throw-in, but only for the team taking the throw.

Support Refers to offensive or defensive assistance provided by a teammate. Offensively, a player may provide support to a marked teammate with the ball by taking a position in an open space to receive a support pass. Defensively, a player may provide support to a teammate who is marking an attacker with the ball by taking a ready position behind the teammate.

Support Foot (see **Planted Foot**)

Support Pass (see **Support**)

Sweeper This player is a free back behind the last line of defenders (see **Libero**). The primary responsibilities of the sweeper are to provide support for the defender at the point of the attack and to intercept passes that penetrate the defense.

Swerved Ball (see **Banana** and **Bending the Ball**)

Switch A switch occurs when two players change assignments and/or positions.

System (System of Play) Amalgamation of style of play and team formation (see **Style of Play** and **Formation**). Note that two teams, using the same team formation, may demonstrate a drastically different system of play because of the differences in their styles of play. Similarly, the overall systems of play of two teams using different formations may be relatively alike.

Tackle (Tackling) Refers to the various individual defensive techniques in which the feet are used to dispossess an opponent of the ball or to interfere with the intended play.

Tactics Offensive and defensive decisions, whether performed by one player, in combination with a few teammates, or by an entire team, become tactics when they are used with the intent to create a strategic advantage in play.

Take a Dive (Taking a Dive) Refers to the acting displayed by a player pretending to be fouled by an opponent. It usually involves falling or diving to the ground in response to contact by an opponent. A player who is judged by the referee as taking a dive can be given a caution for unsportsmanlike behavior.

Take-Over Run (see **Cross-Over Run**)

Techniques The basic individual movements used both offensively and defensively in soccer (e.g., inside of the foot kick, block tackle, and dribbling the ball with the outside of the foot).

Ten Yards (10 Yards) Refers to the minimum distance from the ball that defenders are permitted during the taking of any free kick, with the exception of an indirect free kick that is located less than 10 yards from the defending team's goal line.

Three-Man System A standard officiating system in which one referee and two linespersons are used.

Through Pass A forward pass that penetrates the defense line and leads the receiver into the space behind the defense.

Throw-In Refers to the method of restarting play after the ball has gone out of bounds over the touch line. A goal cannot be scored directly from a throw-in.

"Time" This is a call used to inform a teammate with the ball or about to receive the ball that defenders will not be immediately marking.

Toe Ball A kick in which contact with the ball is made only with the toe of a shoe.

Toe Poke An individual technique for tackling the ball away from an opponent in which the foot is extended to reach the ball and poke it away with the toe of the shoe.

Total Football (Total Soccer) A system employed by the Dutch National Team in the 1974 World Cup. This system requires all players to possess a high level of both offensive and defensive skills because they freely change positions and responsibilities during a match.

Touch This term is used in three different ways. (a) To describe a fine sense of control some players have in maneuvering the ball. (b) The area beyond the side lines of the field. A ball that is "into touch" can be touched with the hands to throw it back into play. (c) The term "touch" is combined with a number to describe how many contacts a player has with the ball during a possession. For example, a player that "two touches" the ball receives the ball and then kicks it on the next touch (see **First Time**).

Touch Line   A side boundary (side line) of the field that extends from one goal line to another.

Trap (Trapping)   This term has become outdated and replaced by receiving. A term generally used to define the process of receiving a soccer ball. The term "trap" is commonly combined with a body part to identify the body segment used to gain control of the ball (e.g., thigh trap, chest trap, sole of the foot trap).

Trip (Tripping)   A penal foul that occurs when players use their feet and legs to unbalance or attempt to unbalance an opponent.

Two-Man System   A modified system of officiating in which two referees on the field have legal authority in controlling play.

Up Field   (see **Down Field**)

Volley   A kick made on an air ball (e.g., side volley, instep volley).

Wall (Defensive Wall, Human Wall)   A barrier formed by two or more defenders standing side-by-side to assist their goalkeeper in defending against a free kick.

Wall Pass   A one touch return of a pass to a player who sprints into open space to receive the ball back. The player making the return pass is used as a wall to rebound (pass) the ball back.

Warning   An admonishment given to a player who has infringed in some way upon the rules. Referees will sometimes use a warning before giving a caution (showing a yellow card) to a player.

Weak Foot   The non-dominant foot of a player.

Weak Side   Refers to the side of the field opposite to where the ball is located.

Width   An offensive principle of play in which attacking players take up positions spread across the field from one touch line to another. This type of positioning spreads the defense and creates more open space.

Wing (Winger)   A player on either end of the halfback or forward line may be called a winger (see **Outside Forward, Outside Left,** and **Outside Right**).

World Cup   The official world championship of soccer. It is sanctioned by FIFA and held once every four years.

Wrong Side of the Ball   Refers to the positioning of defenders between their opponent's goal and the ball. This positioning is opposite to goalside positioning.

Zone   A system of defense in which players are assigned to protect specific areas of the field.

References

Youth Soccer: A Complete Handbook
Eugene W. Brown, Ph.D., Editor

A comprehensive guide for youth soccer coaches. Covers virtually every aspect of the game. 570 pages, hundreds of illustrations. The most comprehensive youth soccer coaching book available. $30.

Training Nutrition: The Diet and Nutrition Guide for Peak Performance
Edmund R. Burke, Ph.D., and Jacqueline R. Berning, Ph.D., R.D.

A no-nonsense guide to the best diet for peak performance. Covers the basics of diet and nutrition as they relate to athletic performance. Written by an exercise physiologist and nutritionist with years of experience working with athletes at every level. Easy to read, understand, and implement. 164 pages, $20.

Your Injury: A Common Sense Guide to Sports Injuries
Merrill A. Ritter, M.D., and Marjorie J. Albohm, A.T., C.

Perfect for the weekend athlete or active person. A well-illustrated, 188 page guide to 95 of the most common sports-related injuries. Provides complete descriptions, symptoms, and recommendations for treatment. $16.

Sports and Recreation for the Disabled, 2nd Edition
Michael J. Paciorek, Ph.D., and Jeffery A. Jones, M.P.E.

A comprehensive guide to 54 sports and recreational opportunities for the disabled, from all-terrain vehicles to wrestling. This 452 page book provides a wealth of information for persons seeking comprehensive information on sports and recreation for the disabled. $20.

The United States Olympic Committee *Sports Education Series*

This unique series of books—one for each Olympic sport—provides parents and youth coaches with the best available information on how to assure that young participants derive the best outcome from their sport experience.

Contact:

Cooper Publishing Group
1048 Summit Drive
Carmel, IN 46032
(317) 574-9338

APPENDIX A
United States Olympic Committee
Coaching Ethics Code

TABLE OF CONTENTS

COACHING ETHICS CODE

INTRODUCTION

This Ethics Code is intended to provide standards of professional conduct that can be applied by the USOC and its member organizations that choose to adopt them. Whether or not a coach has violated the Ethics Code does not by itself determine whether he or she is legally liable in a court action, whether a contract is enforceable, or whether other legal consequences occur. These results are based on legal rather than ethical rules. However, compliance with or violation of the Ethics Code may be admissible as evidence in some legal proceedings, depending on the circumstances.

This Code is intended to provide both the general principles and the decision rules to cover most situations encountered by coaches. It has as its primary goal the welfare and protection of the individuals and groups with whom coaches work. This Code also provides a common set of values upon which coaches build their professional work. It is the individual responsibility of each coach to aspire to the highest possible standards of conduct. Coaches respect and protect human and civil rights, and do not knowingly participate in or condone unfair discriminatory practices.

GENERAL PRINCIPLES

Principle A: Competence

Coaches strive to maintain high standards of excellence in their work. They recognize the boundaries of their particular competencies and the limitations of their expertise. They provide only those services and use only those techniques for which they are qualified by education, training, or experience. In those areas in which recognized professional standards do not yet exist, coaches exercise careful judgement and take appropriate precautions to protect the welfare of those with whom they work. They maintain knowledge of relevant scientific and professional information related to the services they render, and they recognize the need for ongoing education. Coaches make appropriate use of scientific, professional, technical, and administrative resources.

Principle B: Integrity

Coaches seek to promote integrity in the practice of coaching. Coaches are honest, fair, and respectful of others. In describing or reporting their qualifications, services, products, or fees, they do not make statements that are false, misleading, or deceptive. Coaches strive to be aware of their own belief systems, values, needs, and limitations and the effect of these on their work. To the extent feasible, they attempt to clarify for relevant parties the roles they are performing and to function appropriately in accordance with those roles. Coaches avoid improper and potentially harmful dual relationships.

Principle C: Professional Responsibility

Coaches uphold professional standards of conduct, clarify their professional roles and obligations, accept appropriate responsibility for their behavior, and adapt their methods to the needs of different athletes. Coaches consult with, refer to, or cooperate with other professionals and institutions to the extent needed to serve the best interest of their athletes, or other recipients of their services. Coaches' moral standards and conduct are personal matters to the same degree as is true for any other person, except when coaches' conduct may compromise their professional responsibilities or reduce the public's trust in the coaching profession and coaches. Coaches are concerned about the ethical compliance of their colleagues' professional conduct. When appropriate, they consult with colleagues in order to prevent or avoid unethical conduct.

Principle D: Respect for Participants* and Dignity

Coaches respect the fundamental rights, dignity, and worth of all participants. Coaches are aware of cultural, individual, and role differences, including those due to age, gender, race, ethnicity, national origin, religion, sexual orientation, disability, language, and socioeconomic status. Coaches try to eliminate the effect on their work of biases based on those factors, and they do not knowingly participate in or condone unfair discriminatory practices.

Principle E: Concern for Others' Welfare

Coaches seek to contribute to the welfare of those with whom they interact professionally. In their professional actions, coaches consider the welfare and rights of their athletes and other participants. When conflicts occur among coaches' obligations or concerns, they attempt to resolve these conflicts and to perform their roles in a responsible fashion that avoids or minimizes harm. Coaches are sensitive to differences in power between themselves and others, and they do not exploit or mislead other people during or after professional relationships.

Principle F: Responsible Coaching

Coaches are aware of their professional responsibilities to the community and the society in which they work and live. They apply and make public their knowledge of sport in order to contribute to human welfare. Coaches try to avoid misuse of their work. Coaches comply with the law and encourage the development of law and policies that serve the interest of sport. They are encouraged to contribute a portion of their professional time for little or no personal advantage.

ETHICAL STANDARDS

1. GENERAL STANDARDS

These General Standards are applicable to the professional activities of all coaches.

* =Participants: those taking part in sport (athletes and their family members, coaches, officials, volunteers, administrators, and spectators)

1.01 Applicability of the Ethics Code

While many aspects of personal behavior and private activities seem far removed from official duties of coaching, all coaches should be sensitive to their position as role models for their athletes. Private activities perceived as immoral or illegal can influence the coaching environment and coaches are encouraged to observe the standards of this Ethics Code consistently.

1.02 Boundaries of Competence

(a) Coaches provide services only within the boundaries of their competence, based on their education, training, supervised experience, or appropriate professional experience.

(b) Coaches provide services involving new techniques only after first undertaking appropriate study, training, supervision, and/or consultation from persons who are competent in those areas or techniques.

(c) In those emerging areas in which generally recognized standards for preparatory training do not yet exist, coaches nevertheless take reasonable steps to ensure the competence of their work and to protect athletes and other participants from harm.

1.03 Maintaining Expertise

Coaches maintain a reasonable level of awareness of current scientific and professional information in their fields of activity, and undertake ongoing efforts to maintain competence in the skills they use.

1.04 Basis for Professional Judgements

Coaches rely on scientifically and professionally derived knowledge when making professional judgements or when engaging in professional endeavors.

1.05 Describing the Nature and Results of Coaching Services

When coaches provide services to an individual, a group, or an organization, they provide, using language that is reasonably understandable to the recipient of those services, appropriate information beforehand about the nature of such services and appropriate information later about results and conclusions.

1.06 Respecting Others

Coaches respect the rights of others to hold values, attitudes and opinions that differ from their own.

1.07 Nondiscrimination

Coaches do not engage in discrimination based on age, gender, race, ethnicity, national origin, religion, sexual orientation, disability, language, socioeconomic status, or any basis proscribed by law.

1.08 Sexual Harassment

(a) Coaches do not engage in sexual harassment. Sexual harassment is sexual solicitation, physical advances, or verbal or nonverbal conduct that is sexual in nature, and that either:

1. is unwelcome, is offensive, or creates a hostile environment, and the coach knows or is told this;
2. is sufficiently severe or intense to be abusive to a reasonable person in the context. Sexual harassment can consist of a single intense or severe act or of multiple persistent or pervasive acts.

(b) Coaches accord sexual-harassment complainants and respondents dignity and respect. Coaches do not participate in denying an athlete the right to participate based upon their having made, or their being the subject of, sexual harassment charges.

1.09 Other Harassment

Coaches do not engage in behavior that is harassing or demeaning to persons with whom they interact in their work based on factors such as those persons' age, gender, race, ethnicity, national origin, religion, sexual orientation, disability, language, or socioeconomic status.

1.10 Personal Problems and Conflicts

(a) Coaches recognize that their personal problems and conflicts may interfere with their effectiveness. Accordingly, they refrain from undertaking an activity when they know or should know that their personal problems are likely to lead to harm to athletes or other participants to whom they may owe a professional obligation.

(b) In addition, coaches have an obligation to be alert to signs of, and to obtain assistance for, their personal problems at an early stage, in order to prevent significantly impaired performance.

(c) When coaches become aware of personal problems that may interfere with their performing work-related duties adequately, they take appropriate measures, such as obtaining professional consultation or assistance, and determine whether they should limit, suspend, or terminate their work-related duties.

1.11 Avoiding Harm

Coaches take reasonable steps to avoid harming their athletes or other participants, and to minimize harm where it is foreseeable and unavoidable.

1.12 Misuse of Coaches' Influence

Because coaches' professional judgements and actions may affect the lives of others, they are alert to guard against personal, financial, social, organizational, or political factors that might lead to misuse of their influence.

1.13 Multiple Relationships

(a) In many communities and situations, it may not be feasible or reasonable for coaches to avoid social or other nonprofessional contacts with athletes and other participants. Coaches must always be sensitive to the potential harmful effects of other contacts on their work and on those persons with whom they deal. A coach refrains from entering into or promising another personal, professional, financial, or other relationship with such persons if it appears likely that such a relationship reasonably might impair the coach's objectivity or otherwise interfere with the coach's effectively performing his or her functions as a coach, or might harm or exploit the other party.

(b) Likewise, whenever feasible, a coach refrains from taking on professional obligations when preexisting relationships would create a risk of such harm.

(c) If a coach finds that, due to unforeseen factors, a potentially harmful multiple relationship has arisen, the coach attempts to resolve it with due regard for the best interests of the affected person and maximal compliance with the Ethics Code.

1.14 Exploitative Relationships

(a) Coaches do not exploit athletes or other participants over whom they have supervisory, evaluative, or other authority.

(b) Coaches do not engage in sexual/romantic relationships with athletes or other participants over whom the coach has evaluative, direct, or indirect authority, because such relationships are likely to impair judgement or be exploitative.

1.15 Consultations and Referrals

When indicated and professionally appropriate, coaches cooperate with other professionals in order to serve their athletes or other participants effectively and appropriately.

1.16 Delegation to and Supervision of Subordinates

(a) Coaches delegate to their employees, supervisees, and assistants only those responsibilities that such persons can reasonably be expected to perform competently, on the basis of their education, training, or experience, either independently or with the level of supervision being provided.

(b) Coaches provide proper training and supervision to their employees or supervisees and take reasonable steps to see that such persons perform services responsibly, competently, and ethically.

1.17 Fees and Financial Arrangements

(a) As early as is feasible in a professional relationship, the coach and the athlete or other participants reach an agreement specifying the compensation and the billing arrangements.

(b) Coaches do not exploit recipients of services or payers with respect to fees.

(c) Coaches' fee practices are consistent with law.

(d) Coaches do not misrepresent their fees.

(e) If limitations to services can be anticipated because of limitations in financing, this is discussed with the athlete or other participant as appropriate.

2. ADVERTISING AND OTHER PUBLIC STATEMENTS

2.01 Definition of Public Statements

Coaches comply with the Ethics Code in public statements relating to their professional services, products, or publications.

2.02 Statements by Others

(a) Coaches who engage others to create or place public statements that promote their professional practice, products, or activities retain professional responsibility for such statements.

(b) In addition, coaches make reasonable efforts to prevent others whom they do not control (such as employers, publishers, sponsors, organizational clients, and representatives of the print or broadcast media) from making deceptive statements concerning the coach or his professional activities.

(c) If coaches learn of deceptive statements about their work made by others, coaches make reasonable efforts to correct such statements.

(d) Coaches do not compensate members of press, radio, television, or other communication media in return for publicity in a news item.

(e) A paid advertisement relating to the coach's activities must be identified as such, unless it is already apparent from the context.

2.03 Avoidance of False or Deceptive Statements

Coaches do not make public statements that are false, deceptive, misleading, or fraudulent, either because of what they state, convey or suggest, or because of what they omit, concerning their work activities or those of persons or organizations with which they are affiliated. As examples (and not in limitation) of this standard, coaches do not make false or deceptive statements concerning

1. their training, experience, or competence;
2. their academic degrees;
3. their credentials;
4. their institutional or association affiliations;
5. their services;
6. the basis for, or results or degree of success of their services; or
7. their fees.

2.04 Media Presentations

When coaches provide advice or comment by means of public lectures, demonstrations, radio or television programs, prerecorded tapes, printed articles, mailed material, or other media, they take reasonable precautions to ensure that the statements are consistent with this Ethics Code.

2.05 Testimonials

Coaches do not solicit testimonials from current athletes or other participants who, because of their particular circumstances, are vulnerable to undue influence.

2.06 Recruiting

Coaches do not engage, directly or through agents, in uninvited in-person solicitation of business from actual or potential athletes or other participants who, because of their particular circumstances, are vulnerable to undue influence. However, this does not preclude recruiting athletes deemed eligible by appropriate governing bodies.

3. TRAINING ATHLETES

3.01 Structuring the Relationship

(a) Coaches discuss with athletes as early as is feasible appropriate issues, such as the nature and anticipated course of training, fees, and confidentiality..

(b) When the coach's work with athletes will be supervised, the above discussion includes that fact, and the name of the supervisor.

(c) When the coach is uncertified the athlete is informed of that fact.

(d) Coaches make reasonable efforts to answer athletes' questions and to avoid apparent misunderstandings about training. Whenever possible, coaches provide oral and/or written information, using language that is reasonably understandable to the athlete.

3.02 Family Relationships

(a) When a coach agrees to provide services to several persons who have a relationship (such as parents and children), the coach attempts to clarify at the outset

1. which of the individuals are athletes and
2. the relationship the coach will have with each person. This clarification includes the role of the coach and the probable uses of the services provided.

(b) As soon as it becomes apparent that the coach may be called on to perform potentially conflicting roles (such as intermediary between parents and children or sibling teammates), the coach attempts to clarify and adjust, or withdraw from, roles appropriately.

3.03 Providing Coaching Services To Those Served by Others

In deciding whether to offer or provide services to those already receiving coaching services elsewhere, coaches carefully consider the potential athlete's welfare. The coach discusses these issues with the athlete or another legally authorized person on behalf of the athlete, in order to minimize the risk of confusion and conflict.

3.04 Sexual Intimacies with Current Athletes

Coaches do not engage in sexual intimacies with current athletes.

3.05 Coaching Former Sexual Partners

Coaches do not coach athletes with whom they have engaged in sexual intimacies.

3.06 Sexual Intimacies with Former Athletes

(a) Coaches should not engage in sexual intimacies with a former athlete for at least two years after cessation or termination of professional services.

(b) Because sexual intimacies with a former athlete are so frequently harmful to the athlete, and because such intimacies undermine public confidence in the coaching profession and thereby deter the public's use of needed service, coaches do not engage in sexual intimacies with former athletes even after a two-year interval except in the most unusual circumstances. The coach who engages in such activity after the two years following cessation or termination of the coach-athlete relationship bears the burden of demonstrating that there has been no exploitation, in light of all relevant factors, including:

1. the amount of time that has passed since the coach-athlete relationship terminated,
2. the circumstances of termination,
3. the athlete's personal history,
4. the athlete's current mental status,
5. the likelihood of adverse impact on the athlete
6. any statements or actions made by the coach during the course of the athlete-coach relationship suggesting or inviting the possibility of a post-termination sexual or romantic relationship with the athlete or coach.

3.07 Drug-Free Sport

(a) Coaches do not tolerate the use of performance-enhancing drugs and support athletes' efforts to be drug-free.

3.08 Alcohol & Tobacco

(a) Coaches discourage the use of alcohol and tobacco in conjunction with athletic events or victory celebrations at playing sites and forbid use of alcohol by minors.

(b) Coaches refrain from tobacco and alcohol use while they are coaching and make every effort to avoid their use while in the presence of their athletes.

3.09 Interruption of Services

(a) Coaches make reasonable efforts to plan for training in the event that coaching services are interrupted by factors such as the coach's illness, death, unavailability, or relocation or by the client's relocation or financial limitations.

(b) When entering into employment or contractual relationships, coaches provide for orderly and appropriate resolution of responsibility for athlete training in the event that the employment or contractual relationship ends, with paramount consideration given to the welfare of the athlete.

3.10 Terminating the Professional Relationship

(a) Coaches terminate a professional relationship when it becomes reasonably clear that the athlete no longer needs the service, is not benefiting, or is being harmed by continued service.

(b) Prior to termination, for whatever reason, except where precluded by the athlete's conduct, the coach discusses the athlete's views and needs, provides appropriate pre-termination counseling, suggests alternative service providers as appropriate, and takes other reasonable steps to facilitate transfer of responsibility to another provider if the athlete needs one immediately.

4. TRAINING SUPERVISION

4.01 Design of Training Programs

Coaches who are responsible for training programs for other coaches seek to ensure that the programs are competently designed, provide the proper experiences, and meet the requirements for certification or other goals for which claims are made by the program.

4.02 Descriptions of Training Programs

(a) Coaches responsible for training programs for other coaches seek to ensure that there is a current and accurate description of the program content, training goals and objectives, and requirements that must be met for satisfactory completion of the program. This information must be readily available to all interested parties.

(b) Coaches seek to ensure that statements concerning their training programs are accurate and not misleading.

4.03 Accuracy and Objectivity in Coaching

(a) When engaged in coaching, coaches present information accurately and with a reasonable degree of objectivity.

(b) When engaged in coaching, coaches recognize the power they hold over athletes and therefore make reasonable efforts to avoid engaging in conduct that is personally demeaning to athletes and other participants.

4.04 Assessing Athlete Performance

(a) In coach-athlete relationships, coaches establish an appropriate process for providing feedback to athletes.

(b) Coaches evaluate athletes on the basis of their actual performance on relevant and established program requirements.

4.05 Honoring Commitments

Coaches take reasonable measures to honor all commitments they have made to athletes.

5. TEAM SELECTION

(a) Coaches perform evaluations or team selection only within the context of a defined professional relationship.

(b) Coaches' assessments, recommendations, reports, and evaluative statements used to select team members are based on information and techniques sufficient to provide appropriate substantiation for their findings.

6. RESOLVING ETHICAL ISSUES

6.01 Familiarity With Ethics Code

Coaches have an obligation to be familiar with this Ethics Code, other applicable ethics codes, and their application to the coaches' work. Lack of awareness or misunderstanding of an ethical standard is not itself a defense to a charge of unethical conduct.

6.02 Confronting Ethical Issues

When a coach is uncertain whether a particular situation or course of action would violate the Ethics Code, the coach ordinarily consults with other coaches knowledgeable about ethical issues, with NGB or USOC ethics committees, or with other appropriate authorities in order to choose a proper response.

6.03 Conflicts Between Ethics and Organizational Demands

If the demands of an organization with which coaches are affiliated conflict with this Ethics Code, coaches clarify the nature of the conflict, make known their commitment to the Ethics Code, and to the extent feasible, seek to resolve the conflict in a way that permits the fullest adherence to the Ethics Code.

6.04 Informal Resolution of Ethical Violations

When coaches believe that there may have been an ethical violation by another coach, they attempt to resolve the issue by bringing it to the attention of that individual if an informal resolution appears appropriate and when intervention does not violate any athlete rights that may be involved.

6.05 Reporting Ethical Violations

If an apparent ethical violation is not appropriate for informal resolution under Standard 6.04 or is not resolved properly in that fashion, coaches take further action appropriate to the situation, unless such action conflicts with athlete rights in ways that cannot be resolved. Such action might include referral to NGB or USOC committees on professional ethics.

6.06 Cooperating With Ethics Committees

Coaches cooperate in ethics investigations, proceedings, and resulting requirements of the USOC and any NGB to which they belong. Failure to cooperate is itself an ethics violation.

6.07 Improper Complaints

Coaches do not file or encourage the filing of ethics complaints that are frivolous and are intended to harm the respondent rather than to protect the public.

7. PROCESS RELATING TO VIOLATION OF CODE

7.01

The coach acknowledges that this Ethics Code is administered under the authority of their NGB or other responsible organization and that a violation of this Code subjects the coach to the processes of the NGB or other such organization required to be provided in the event of disciplinary action. The NGB or other such organization acknowledges that all violations of the Ethics Code will be reviewed for possible disciplinary action and it will provide a written report to the USOC on all reviews and actions.

7.02

In the event that a violation of the Ethics Code occurs during an authorized U.S. Olympic Training Center activity, USOC may, as landlord of the facility, take action separate and independent from that of the NGB or member of the USOC in order to protect its interests and those of athletes, coaches and others at the location.

7.03

Any action taken by an NGB or member of the USOC which affects the opportunity of a coach to participate in "protected" competition as defined in th USOC Constitution shall be entitled to processes assured under the USOC Constitution and the Amateur Sports Act of 1978. This includes process within the NGB, the USOC and the American Arbitration Association.

7.04

If the violation of the Ethics Code occurs while a member of a USOC team or event, the coach and NGB acknowledge that the USOC may institute its own pro-

ceeding regarding the violation, which action shall not restrict the ability or obligation of the NGB to take its own separate and independent action.

7.05

In the event that a coach is found to have violated the Ethics Code, such action is separate and apart from any other legal consequences which may occur as a result of the art.

ACKNOWLEDGEMENTS

This Coaching Code of Ethics is the result of the work of many people and committees. The approach, structure, and contents of this code were inspired by the Ethical Principles of Psychologists and Code of Conduct, December 1992 (American Psychological Association, Vol. 47, No. 12, 1597-1611). Many of the ideas for these ethical standards were drawn from numerous other codes. The most significant of these were developed by the Coaching Association of Canada. The British Institute of Sport Coaches, and the NCAA. In particular, the USOC would like to thank:

USOC Coaching Committee, Ray Essick, Chair
USOC Ethics Oversight Committee, Harry Groves, Chair
USOC Games Preparation and Services Committee, Joe Kearney, Chair
USOC Training Centers Committee, Mike Jacki, Chair
USOC Vice President Michael B. Lenard
USOC General Counsel Ronald T. Rowan

APPENDIX B
United States Youth Soccer
Association Coaches' Code of Ethics

The overall responsibility of any coach is to create a safe, fun filled, learning environment.

With this basic premise established, USYSA has developed the following Coaches' Code of Ethics that addresses three areas:

1. SAFETY
2. PLAYER DEVELOPMENT
3. ETHICS

SAFETY

1. My first responsibility is the health and safety of all participants.
2. It is recommended that coaches become certified in basic first aid and are aware of their club, league or state requirements in this area.
3. Be prepared to handle first aid situations as well as medical emergencies at all practices and games, both home and away;
   —have and know how to use a properly supplied first aid kit/ice
   —911 emergency procedures/telephone location
   —location of nearest emergency medical facilities
   —always carry emergency medical release forms and team safety and information cards
   —follow up all injuries with parents/guardians.
4. Know and understand the Laws of the Game.
5. Inspect players equipment and field conditions for safety reasons.
6. Utilize proper teaching and instructing of players regarding safe techniques and methods of play.
7. Implement appropriate training programs to make sure players are fit for practice and competition.
8. Supervise and control your players so as to avoid injury situations.

PLAYER DEVELOPMENT

1. Develop the child's overall appreciation of the game.
2. Keep winning and losing in proper perspective.
3. Be sensitive to each child's developmental needs.
4. Educate the players to the technical, tactical, physical and psychological demands of the game for their level.
5. Implement rule and equipment modifications according to the players age group.
6. Allow players to experience all positions.
7. Players need to have fun and receive positive feedback.
8. Practices should be conducted in the spirit of enjoyment and learning.
9. Provide the appropriate number of training sessions and games according to the players stage of development.
10. Strive to help each player reach his/her full potential and be prepared to move on to the next stage of development.

ETHICS

1. Strive to maintain integrity within our sport.
2. Know and follow all the rules and policies set forth by clubs, leagues, state and national associations.
3. Work in the spirit of cooperation with officials, administrators, coaches and spectators to provide the *participants* with the maximum opportunity to develop.
4. Be a positive role model.
5. Set the standard for sportsmanship with opponents, referees, administrators and spectators.
6. Keep sport in proper perspective with education.
7. Encourage moral and social responsibility.
8. Just say no to drugs and alcohol.
9. Coach should continue his/her own education in the sport.

138

THE YOUNG PLAYERS OF TODAY
WILL BE OUR
STARS OF TOMORROW!

Please help support U.S. Soccer's National Teams Programs.

YES! I want to support U.S. Soccer's National Teams Programs.
Enclosed is my donation of:

Gold Medal Level _____ $500

Silver Medal Level _____ $250

Bronze Medal Level _____ $100

_____ $50

_____ $25

_____ Other $ _____

Please make checks payable to:

U.S. Soccer Federation, Inc
c/o U.S. Soccer
Soccer House
1801-1811 S. Prairie Avenue
Chicago, IL 60616

**All donations will be used to support our
U.S. National Soccer Teams Programs and are tax deductible.**

Thank you for your support.